The Future of Korea–Japan Relations: Proceedings of the Hudson Institute/East Asian Security Study Group Conference, 1997

The Future of Korea–Japan Relations:

Proceedings of the Hudson Institute/East Asian Security Study Group Conference, 1997

Supported by the Center for Global Partnership of the Japan Foundation

Robert Dujarric, editor

ISBN: 1-55813-080-2

The views in this book are solely the views of the author. No opinions, statements of fact, or conclusions contained in this document can be properly attributed to Hudson Institute, its staff, its members, its contracted agencies, or the other institutions with which the author is affiliated.

Printed in the United States of America.

For media and speaking engagement purposes contact:
Hudson Institute
Herman Kahn Center
5395 Emerson Way
Indianapolis, IN 46226, U.S.A.
Phone: 317-545-1000
Fax: 317-545-9639
www.hudson.org
info@hudson.org

For more information about obtaining additional copies of this or other Hudson Institute publications:
Hudson Institute
PO Box 486
Westfield, IN 46074
888-554-1325
Fax: 317-867-0725
Order online at www.hudson.org

Contents

List of Acronyms

APEC	Asia-Pacific Economic Cooperation
ARF	ASEAN regional forum
ASEAN	Association of Southeast Asian Nations
ASW	Anti-Submarine Warfare
CBM	Confidence Building Measures
CFR	Council on Foreign Relations
CMEA	Council on Mutual Economic Assistance
CSCAP	Council for Security Cooperation in the Asian Pacific
DMZ	Demilitarized Zone (between North and South Korea)
DPRK	Democratic People's Republic of Korea (North)
EEZ	Exclusive Economic Zone
FPDA	Five Power Defense Agreement
GDP	Gross Domestic Product
IADS	Integrated Air-Defense System
IAEA	International Atomic Energy Agency
IMF	International Monetary Fund
JMSDF	Japanese Maritime Self-Defense Force
JSDF	Japanese Self-Defense Forces
LWR	Light Water Reactor
MIO	Maritime Interdiction Operation
MNC	Multinational Naval Cooperation
MNCO	Multinational Naval Cooperation Options
NATO	North Atlantic Treaty Organization
NDPO	National Defense Program Outline

NEACD	Northeast Asia Cooperation Dialogue
NEASED	Northeast Asian Security Dialogue
NEO	Noncombatant Evacuation Operation
ROK	Republic of Korea (South)
ROKN	ROK Navy
SACO	Special Action Committee on Facilities and Areas in Okinawa
SAR	Search and Rescue
SLOC	Sea Lines of Communication
SOP	Standard Operating Procedures
SRI	Stanford Research Institute
STANAVFORPAC–Training	Standing Naval Force Pacific–Training
UNOSOM	UN peacekeeping operation, Mozambique
UNPKO	United Nations Peace-Keeping Operations
UNTAC	UN Peacekeeping Operation, Cambodia
WMD	Weapons of Mass Destruction

Introduction

On December 5–6, 1997, Hudson Institute and the East Asian Security Study Group held a conference on Japan and Korea's future. The focus of the conference was to survey the state of Japanese-Korean relations and to analyze how they would evolve in the future.

In the three and a half years since the symposium took place, the pace of the improvement of Korean-Japanese relations has been dramatic. Very few observers in late 1997, even the most optimistic ones, would have predicted that relations between the two nations would improve as rapidly as they did. Though much remains to be done, the trend line has been very impressive.

We hope that these essays will help scholars and policymakers gain a better understanding of the issues surrounding ties between Japan and Korea.

We would like to express our great appreciation for the Center for Global Partnership of the Japan Foundation, which generously funded this conference and provided first-class conference facilities at its headquarters in Tokyo. Professor Izumi Hajime of the University of Shizuoka and the East Asian Security Study Group was able to help us bring some of Japan's best scholars to participate in this conference. F. R. Ruskin deserves our special thanks for her editing efforts.

Robert Dujarric
Hudson Institute

Security of Northeast Asia Following Korean Unification

By Yamaguchi Noboru,
Major General, Japan Ground Self-Defense Forces*

When we try to assess long-term security of Northeast Asia, we must confront the issues associated with Korean unification. During the process of unification, a variety of scenarios have been examined, each of them raising a set of serious questions. From the perspective of regional security, these questions can be summarized into four major elements:

1. What are the geopolitical implications of unification? What is the political direction of a unified Korea?
2. What are the economic implications of unification?
3. What are the military implications of unification? What is the military structure of a unified Korea? Will the U.S. forces remain in Korea after unification?
4. How will the two Koreas be unified? Violently or peacefully? Will there be any upheaval in the North, either internal or extending beyond its borders?

The answers to these questions will affect security throughout the region. Since the issues they raise are interdependent, discussion of them is complicated. And although answering them is extremely diffi-

* *The views expressed are those of the author and do not necessarily represent the views of the Ground Self-Defense Forces or any other Japanese government organization.*

cult or well nigh impossible, it is important to discuss the implications of these questions and what factors determine the answers to the questions. The following sections will examine these questions and try to draw policy recommendations for the United States and Japan.

Geopolitical Implications

The Korean Peninsula is located between major powers: the United States, Japan, China, and Russia. The interests of these major powers have been intersecting with the two Koreas in a complicated manner. Throughout the history of Japan, the peninsula has been the site of a power struggle with the continental powers, particularly with China in the earlier years and Russia in the early twentieth century.[1] The most serious strategic concern for Japan in the past has been the defense of its western flank against threats from the continent through the Korean Peninsula. During the first half of this century, the peninsula was a route through which Japan could expand its influence to the continent and secure its lifelines to Manchuria. After World War II, the 38th parallel became the point of balance not only between the West and the East in a Cold War context, but also between maritime powers (the United States and Japan) and continental powers (China and Russia) in a geopolitical context.[2] Therefore, Japan has been able to enjoy the secured western flank at the expense of the United States and the Republic of Korea (ROK.)

The strategic atlas of the region after unification may differ significantly from the current one. The political direction of a unified Korea, particularly its relations with major powers, will be a major determinant of the nature of this strategic atlas. Relations between the major powers will also be key factors in this context. Although it is difficult to sum up the geostrategic implications of unification, several important points can be made. The geostrategic position of a unified Korea can be defined as that of a typical peninsula state located between maritime and land powers. Unification may increase the significance of these characteristics because of the disappearance of the 38th parallel as the balance point. However, if relations between maritime and continental powers—Sino–U.S./Japan relations in particular—are cooperative, the peninsula may not become the spot for power games.

In addition, the historical view of the peninsula for Japan, China, and Russia as a balance point of their influence has become less significant than in the past. The Korean Peninsula is no longer Japan's lifeline because today's Japan relies on Sea Lines of Communication (SLOCs) to its south. China may also have fewer reasons to expand its influence throughout the peninsula, since its interests in the southern flank seem to be much more significant.[3] So, neither Japan nor China may have to compete with each other over the peninsula. Moreover, Russia does not seem to have the intention or capability to seriously affect the power balance in the peninsula, at least in the coming decades.

Economic Implications

Korean unification involves a merging of two different economies, a rich market economy and a poor controlled economy. This integration seems likely to involve a conversion of the Democratic Peoples Republic of Korea (DPRK) to a market economy. In dealing with the problems associated with this conversion, lessons learned in Germany, Russia, the East European nations, and China may apply. Of course, a radical process may lead to a chaotic situation and may harm the two economies; a gradual and systematic approach is desirable. The following steps should be taken in a synchronized manner:

- Measures to vitalize the DPRK's economy with assistance of the ROK and the international community
- Measures to transform the DPRK's domestic economic system and adapt it to a market economy
- Measures to gradually reduce the barrier between the North and the South, with efforts to reduce the gap between these economies
- Measures to open the DPRK's economy to the neighboring countries and to the entire international community

This broad-based approach will present many challenges and will require time. However, so long as political stability is maintained on the peninsula, such a systematic approach toward conversion of the two economies can be successful.

Among the issues, reducing the gap between the richer and poorer economies seems to be the most problematic. The ROK has 46 million people with some $12,000 gross domestic product (GDP) per capita, while the DPRK has a population of 25 million with less than $1,000 GDP per capita.[4] When unification takes place, two rich South Koreans must feed one poor North Korean whose income is less than one-tenth of theirs. This will be much harder than in the German case where four rich West Germans had to accommodate one East German whose income was one-third to one-half of theirs.[5] This suggests that the South Korean burden may be much heavier than the West German one. Moreover, while West Germany was one of the world's largest economies when Germany was reunited, the ROK's economy is not as powerful.

Although unification poses tough economic problems, certain steps can be taken to alleviate them. First, to make the southern economy powerful enough to accommodate the DPRK, the ROK's current financial difficulties should be solved as soon as possible and the economy of the ROK should be revitalized. Second, to avoid domestic chaos in the north, which may lead to collapse or explosion, North Korea's economy must be sustained. Third, to achieve these conditions, economic and technical assistance of the major powers, Japan and the United States in particular, is essential and must be enlisted. Fourth, to keep up its economic growth after unification, a unified Korea should take the ROK's path as an industrial and trading nation, dependent on a stable market and source of energy and on SLOCs. This implies that the unified Korea will share its vital interests to secure freedom of navigation with the United States and Japan.

Military Implications

The current situation of the Korean Peninsula can be defined as a typical confrontational balance of power with a saturated level of military forces. It is remarkable that some 1.7 million regular forces of the North and the South are densely deployed around the Demilitarized Zone (DMZ).[6] Remarkably, this military level exceeds that of the Cold War, when Pacific nations, including Japan, were keenly concerned with Soviet military buildup in the region. Indeed, the Soviet Union significantly increased its Far East forces in the 1970s and 1980s. However, the maximum number of Soviet troops deployed in the region was about 600,000, thinly deployed from the Sino-Soviet borders through the Maritime Province to Kamchatka. While these 600,000 troops drew keen attention in the region, the troops on the Korean Peninsula, nearly 2 million strong, have rarely been viewed as a potential threat. This is because it was believed the DPRK's one million troops were deterred by the ROK–U.S. alliance. In other words, these 1.7 million troops have been pinned down on the peninsula and canceled out, while providing mutual deterrence.

Along with the geopolitical and economic implications, Korean unification may raise a set of military issues. First, the 1.7 million troops will become irrelevant for regional security after the North-South confrontation disappears. Thus, this excessive level of force should be reduced. This will help the unified Korea's economy by reducing the burden of maintaining such a military level and by making young and high-quality men available to the workforce. Second, since a unified Korea will have direct borders with China and Russia, it should be prepared to secure a border three times wider than the 38th parallel. And, since its dependence on maritime trade will remain, the new Korea should be prepared to protect its SLOCs for the sake of its prosperity. Third, a confrontational balance of power between the North and South has been one of the major factors for mutual deterrence on the peninsula, a fact appreciated by other nations in the region. After unification, this contribution will no longer be meaningful. But, since the unified Korea will continue to depend on the peace and stability of the region and the world as a whole, it may be called upon to participate in the efforts of the international community to maintain regional and global stability. Fourth, it may be necessary to keep domestic order during the transition period. Since political stability on the peninsula will be vital during this period, and can be upset by economic and social changes, the military will be needed as a stabilizing factor within the country. In short, the unified Korea's military forces should be ready to assume various responsibilities:

- They should be prepared to protect Korea's northern borders with China and Russia as the situation requires. A sizable land force will be needed.
- They should contribute to the efforts of maritime powers to secure safety of navigation through the Pacific Ocean and Indian Ocean to the Persian Gulf. For this, a unified Korea's navy should supplement the roles of the U.S. Navy and the Japanese Maritime Self-Defense Force and should cooperate with them.
- They may have to participate in international efforts to keep regional and global peace and stability. The unified Korea's military may be required to dispatch forces abroad for peacekeeping and humanitarian/disaster relief operations. The military may also be invited to participate in implementation of international arms control agreements by sending military specialists for activities such as those that UNSCOM has been conducting in Iraq.
- They should undertake operations to keep internal order throughout the unification and post-unification process, until the domestic situation is settled.

The level and the structure of the forces needed for these measures may be determined mainly by a unified Korea's relationship with the surrounding powers. If Korea has cooperative relations with all the major powers, the force level can be fairly moderate. If it has confrontational relations with any of them, security requirements will be much greater and more complex. For example, competition with navies of the United States and Japan would have a negative impact on the security of Korea's SLOCs, and could harm its economic growth as well. It is also obvious that securing the borders against a hostile China or Russia would pose serious security burdens to the Koreans.

In addition to the structure of military force in a unified Korea, U.S. military presence on the peninsula should be discussed, since the primary mission of deterring the DPRK will no longer be necessary. On the other hand, U.S. presence on the peninsula or in the region will remain necessary in roles such as:

- Providing extended nuclear deterrence for the unified Korea through its physical presence
- Serving as a stabilizing influence on the peninsula, to avoid chaos during the transition period
- Providing reassurance for countries in the region by showing strong, continued commitment to northeast Asia
- Responding to regional crises in the Asian-Pacific
- Alleviating regional concern over the emergence of a hegemonic power such as an expanded China or a remilitarized Japan

Regardless of the necessity, U.S. military presence on the peninsula after the unification will be determined by such factors as the unified Korea's desire to keep U.S. forces in its territory, U.S. public opinion on continued U.S. involvement on the peninsula, and the Chinese attitude toward U.S. military presence in the region. Again, these factors will be affected by the international political climate, particularly the relations between the United States and China.[7] If China is cooperative, it may not oppose the U.S. presence, whereas the United States and Korea may have difficulties legitimizing the presence of U.S. forces in Korea in the absence of a visible threat. On the other hand, if China is hostile, the United States and a unified Korea may be eager to keep forces to deal with a possible enemy, whereas China will have many reasons to oppose U.S. military presence in the region.

Implications of the Unification Process

Among the questions on how the two Koreas will be unified, questions of whether it will involve violence is the most important for regional security. Many have argued that an explosion or an implosion of the North may be what triggers the unification. Regardless of the scenario, violence may pose a tremendous cost to the region both physically and politically. Physically, military conflicts on the peninsula will cost lives, the financial burden of waging war, and severe damage to the infrastructure on the peninsula. In addition, violent unification may complicate the international politics. The nature of the involvement of the United States, China, Russia, and Japan during the unification process, if it is violent, may seriously affect international politics in post-unification Northeast

Asia. For all concerned, avoiding violence during the unification process must be the primary goal.

Certain factors may be critical to keeping the unification process peaceful. To keep mutual deterrence workable, the military balance on the peninsula should be maintained. The key elements for this include continued U.S. military commitment, a strong ROK–U.S. alliance, and Japan's support for the U.S. forces in case of regional contingencies. It is also important to make efforts toward confidence-building and arms control on the peninsula to reduce tensions between the two Koreas and to keep the level of force for mutual deterrence as low as possible. A lower force level will not only reduce the possibility of war but also significantly reduce the burden of maintaining large-scale forces on both sides, so that resources can be allocated to economic preparation for unification. Cooperative, coordinated approaches by the major powers are also important to avoid chaotic or violent unification. To implement the results of the 2+2 talks, consultation with Russia and Japan are the keys. It is essential that China and the United States cooperate in exercising their influence over the DPRK, particularly while North Korea's collapse or explosion remains a possibility.

Future Directions

The implications of Korean unification in the preceding discussion range from negative to constructive outcomes, and we have outlined several factors that are key to making the outcome favorable. Although those factors may be highly scenario-dependent and each of them will be largely determined by other factors, there seem to be some overall directions we can follow to achieve the best results.

First, the relationships among the major powers will be an important influence. It is vital to encourage cooperation among these powers to promote peaceful unification and avoid power struggles that may negatively affect the relationship between the two Koreas. In this context, various bilateral efforts have been made. The United States and Japan have recently strengthened their alliance; Russia and the United States have improved their relationship since the end of the Cold War through various programs such as Partnership for Peace; and China and Russia have been working on the bilateral relationship they have defined as "strategic partners." The remaining questions are Sino–U.S., Sino-Japanese, and perhaps Russo-Japanese relationships. Recent developments in these bilateral relations are promising. The Japanese prime minister visited China and Russia in the latter half of 1997. A variety of military exchange programs between the People's Liberation Army and the Japanese Self-Defense Forces are scheduled in 1998, initiated by Chinese Defense Minister Chi Hao Tian's visit in February and the Ground Self-Defense Force chief's visit to China in March. The Sino–U.S. relationship has also been promoted through various high-level exchanges such as Jiang Ze Min's visit to the United States in October 1997 and Defense Secretary William Cohen's visit to Beijing in January 1998. These initiatives should be followed by continuing efforts by all the players, particularly in a military-to-military context.

More important, there should be an institution that involves all of these major powers. It is urgent that we institutionalize a mechanism by which the United States, China, Japan, and Russia can pursue policy coordination and cooperation. Because all of these major powers have global influence, such a mechanism should not be limited to a Korean context, but should have wider regional or global aims. A formalized quadrilateral scheme is desirable. Toward this end are several options, including an informal quadrilateral forum to prepare for a formal mechanism, or a set of trilateral frameworks, such as one with the United States, Japan, and China that could be expanded or merged to a quadrilateral forum.

Second, the United States, the ROK, and Japan should make strong efforts to maintain mutual deterrence on the peninsula. For this purpose, the United States should strengthen and maintain its alliance with the ROK to keep credible deterrence and defense posture on the peninsula. In the meantime, the U.S.–Japan security alliance should be maintained and strengthened as one of the critical keys. Japan should take immediate steps to enhance its assurance of support to U.S. forces in case of regional contingencies, in accordance with the Defense Guidelines reviewed in 1997. This will not only increase the capability to deal with contingencies, but will also promote deterrence by U.S. forces in the region so that the probability of military conflicts will decrease.

While the United States, the ROK, and Japan will cooperate to deal with contingencies on the peninsula through these two well-established bilateral alliances, a Korean-Japanese bilateral scheme and a trilateral forum of three countries would ensure smoother cooperation. In this context, there have been several positive developments in recent years. Since 1994, working-level dialogues between the ROK and Japan have been held each year, as well as high-level defense talks and mutual port visits of naval vessels.[8] This bilateral defense exchange has promoted mutual understanding and increased the opportunities for future cooperation in security matters. There has also been some development in a trilateral context. In August 1994, scholars, defense officials, foreign office officials, and military officers of the United States, Japan, and South Korea gathered in Hawaii for the first track-two trilateral meeting.

This meeting was transformed to a track-one at the third meeting in June 1996. Defense policy makers, military planners, and diplomats of the three countries have discussed regional security issues and trilateral cooperation for regional stability. This U.S.–JAPAN–ROK Trilateral Meeting should be utilized for future cooperation.

Third, the United States and the ROK also should take steps toward confidence-building and arms control on the peninsula. Currently, there seems to be a fundamental difference between the North and the South about arms control. While the ROK demands confidence building before arms reduction, the DPRK has been insisting on arms reductions first.[9] The first step is to reduce mutual suspicion. In this context, measures for confidence-building and arms reduction need not necessarily be separate. Of course, significant arms reduction will not occur without mutual confidence, but a small arms reduction step may begin to build mutual trust. For example, a unilateral announcement of reduction of obsolete weapons may have a positive impact on the momentum on the bilateral dialogue for arms control, or at the very least it would be a step toward more transparency. The four-party (2+2) talks among the two Koreas, the United States, and China should be utilized for this purpose.

Fourth, the United States and Japan, with the cooperation of China, Russia, and other countries, should support the ROK to make its economy strong enough to accommodate the DPRK's economy. The United States and Japan should also take economic measures to avoid a chaotic situation in the north. Revitalizing the ROK's economy and helping to sustain the livelihood of the North Korean people are the first and most urgent objectives.

Finally, the United States, China, and the two Koreas should prepare for implementation of what the four-party (2+2) talks achieve through the involvement of Japan and Russia. Japan may be called upon for robust economic assistance, while Russia will be invited to exercise its political influence in a positive manner during the process of unification. The involvement of these two countries will be inevitable at some point. Therefore, the four-party talks should be expanded to a 6-party (2+2+2 or 2+4) scheme, perhaps within two to five years.

Conclusion

It is hard to predict what will happen on the peninsula. Meanwhile, whether we can be optimistic or pessimistic about the future depends on what we can do as well as how we analyze the situation. The desirable outcome is a peacefully unified Korea as a prosperous industrial/trading country, which has cooperative relations with its neighboring major powers and plays a constructive role in the regional security. To work toward that resolution, all the players should agree on a set of policies. The United States, China, Japan, and Russia, as well as the two Koreas, should make constructive contributions to the political, economic, and military aspects of unification as has been suggested here. A cooperative and comprehensive approach to the security of the region is needed to ensure a stable future.

Notes

[1] Since the middle of the fourth century, Japan repeatedly intervened in Korean civil wars until 663 when it was decisively beaten in the sea battle against Sino-Shilla allied forces. In the thirteenth century, Mongolian invaders twice almost reached Kyushu Island through the Korean Peninsula. In the late sixteenth century, Japan sent troops twice to the peninsula, but withdrew because the invasions were unsuccessful. For historical perspective on the strategic concern of Japan and China in the Korean Peninsula, see Hisahiko Okazaki, A Grand Strategy for Japanese Defense, (Lanham, MD: University Press of America, 1986).

[2] For Japanese strategists, post-WWII was an exceptional period when they did not have to worry about the security on Japan's western flank, which allowed them to focus on the Soviet threat on their northern flank.

[3] China has shown an interest in the South China Sea, possibly because of oil deposits in the region. For example, China has declared that most of the South China Sea belongs to them by a law enacted in February 1992. Recent Chinese naval modernization has been interpreted as a sign that China is trying to expand its influence southward.

[4] IISS, The Military Balance 1995-1996.

[5] According to The Military Balance 1990–1991 (IISS), West Germany in 1989 had a population of 60,362,000 with some $20,000 GDP per capita, while the East German population was 16,664,000 with $6,000–12,000 GDP per capita.

[6] According to The Military Balance 1997–1998 (IISS), total strength of the armed forces is 1,055,000 for the DPRK and 672,000 for the ROK.

[7] In the latter half of 1997, Chinese security specialists began to show signs of a more relaxed Chinese attitude toward U.S. military presence on the peninsula after unification. In October 1997, a senior researcher of a Chinese think tank close to the government said that China will have no reason to oppose U.S. military presence in the unified Korea if Korea wants it. He also mentioned that as long as the Sino-U.S. relationship is good, a U.S. military presence will not threaten China. Similar comments were made on various occasions from October to December 1997.

[8] Japan Defense Agency, Defense of Japan 1997, p. 87.

[9] The Ministry of National Defense of the Republic of Korea, *Defense White Paper* 1996–1997, pp. 155–156.

International Politics of Korean Reunification:

Reunification Process and Post-Reunification Regional Order in Northeast Asia

By Kim Taehyun,
Graduate School of International Studies
Chung-Ang University in Seoul

Introduction

Fundamentally, reunification of the Korean Peninsula is a matter of international politics. While division itself was a product of international politics, the politics of the global Cold War had by then profoundly shaped and affected the nature and development of inter-Korean relations, thereby constraining any prospect of reunification. Still, the likelihood and process of reunification will surely be affected by how the international political order unfolds in Northeast Asia. In recent years, as reunification has become a more realistic possibility, there is a growing recognition that the manner and process of reunification will have far-reaching repercussions for regional international politics, particularly for relations among the four neighboring major powers—the United

States, China, Japan, and Russia—and for their relationships with a reunified Korea.

This paper examines the relationship between Korean reunification and international politics in northeast Asia. First, it assesses the impact of the emerging regional order in northeast Asia, precipitated by the recent surge of shuttle summit diplomacy by the four major powers, on the likelihood and process of reunification. I begin by constructing four hypothetical types of regional order and exploring the ways in which each order would affect reunification. Second, I examine the impact of reunification on the future of regional order, which is still in flux, by utilizing the literature on reunification scenarios and exploring ways in which each scenario could influence the regional political order. Finally, I will summarize the preceding discussions and derive policy proposals for the governments of surrounding powers as well as for South Korea for achieving peace and stability in both the Korean Peninsula and northeast Asia.

Specifically, this paper argues that a new order built solely around the major powers—be it a neo-bipolar system with the United States and Japan at one pole and China and Russia at the other, a concert of great powers, or a classical balance-of-power system—will negatively affect the likelihood of reunification and be inadequate to meet the challenges associated with the process and consequences. Instead, a new multilateral system of cooperative security in the region would be the more desirable form of regional order, as it would elastically react to any contingencies before, during, and after reunification.

Koreanization and Internationalization of Korean Reunification

The reality of the international aspects of Korean reunification notwithstanding, the term *internationalization* of the Korean question is not popular among South Koreans. The issue of reunification inevitably appeals to their nationalist sentiment. To most Koreans, particularly in recent years, the international nature of the Korean problem has apparently weakened significantly. First, it has been agreed and reiterated between the two Koreas that national reunification shall be pursued autonomously, free from any foreign intervention. Second, the dynamic growth of the South Korean economy, coupled with the weakening of North Korea, has strengthened internal expectations that Koreans themselves can solve the Korean problem. Last, and most important, the Cold War has finally ended.

Indeed, there is no denying that the end of the Cold War has vastly changed the international environment for reunification. In June of 1983, for example, when South Korean Foreign Minister Lee Bom Sok expressed his desire to improve relations with socialist countries, particularly the Soviet Union, the Soviets responded in less than two months by shooting down a civilian airliner and killing more than two hundred civilians. In contrast, the "northern diplomacy" that South Korea has vigorously pursued since the end of the Cold War has proved a remarkable success. Starting with Hungary in 1989, South Korea established diplomatic relations with almost all of the former socialist countries, including the Soviet Union in 1991 and China in 1992.

Yet, *Koreanization* of the Korean problem may turn out to be mere myth, in spite of South Korea's economic and diplomatic successes, for three reasons:

First, the inter-Korean relationship is far from achieving the spirit of reconciliation and cooperation of the post–Cold War world. On the contrary, the two Koreas pursued contradictory policies following the end of the Cold War, and the inter-Korean relationship has now deteriorated to its worst level in many years. After the German example, while many South Koreans did not hide their hope for reunification by absorbing the ailing North, Pyongyang—more fearful of the South than ever—began to name Seoul as its principal enemy in place of the United States.

Pyongyang, for its part, strove for survival by opening up direct talks with the United States, its own version of "northern diplomacy," which may be called "southern diplomacy." Seoul employed *positive* diplomacy to open the doors to allies of Pyongyang, offering inducements made possible by its remarkable economic success. With a failing economy, Pyongyang instead employed *negative* diplomacy, a brinkmanship relying on threats backed by its still formidable military muscle. Although these threats were usually aimed at the United States, which had 37,000 troops stationed along the DMZ, it was in fact South Koreans who suffered the most from them. Accordingly, South Koreans became more hostile and more fearful of North Koreans than ever. The mutual distrust between the two Koreas deepened, and inter-Korean dialogue reached a stalemate. Ironically for the Koreans, the result of the stalemate was the proposal to start four-party talks and to internationalize the Korean question.

Second, the assessment by regional powers raises further questions about Korean autonomy over its reunification. The four-party talks indicate that regional powers, including the United States and China, share a perception that North Korea's situations and policies remain highly unpredictable. The United States has pursued the so-called soft-landing policy with regard to North Korea, believing that North Korea is in such a hopeless condition, like an airplane with major engine failure, that its only hope is to come down gently and avoid a hard crash. Officials in

Washington are concerned that even if North Korea's collapse could lead to reunification of the Korean Peninsula on Seoul's terms, a failing North Korea might either implode or explode, with huge repercussions for the region's stability.

Beijing is equally concerned about the possibility of North Korea's sudden collapse. Not only would China have to bear the major burden of the collapse, but the collapse of North Korea's socialist economy would constitute a political threat to China's politico-economic system and might create a military threat from the U.S.–South Korean allies. The South Korean government also sees the sudden collapse of North Korea as not necessarily desirable because of concerns over reunification costs, and it believes collaboration by neighboring powers in the reunification process is indispensable. In sum, the *process* of reunification became an international issue.

Third and foremost, international politics in Northeast Asia itself is far from the expected pattern of post–Cold War international politics. Despite the intense debate about the future of European security in the post–Cold War era in the early 1990s,[1] the European order seems to follow paths of optimism such as the "liberal end-of-history optimism" or "neo-liberal institutionalism."[2] The balance between optimism and pessimism on the future of East Asia, on the other hand, seems to tilt toward pessimism.[3] The region fosters many sources of conflict and few institutions exist for peaceful conflict resolution, so while Europe is "primed for peace," East Asia is "ripe for rivalry."[4] If this is the case, the region-wide system of conflict can affect and be affected by inter-Korean politics in such a way that the prospect of Korean reunification becomes slimmer, its process becomes more violent, and its consequences become more destabilizing than otherwise.

We can conceptualize the international nature of the Korean question in two ways. The first is the way in which the regional political order, particularly in terms of the relationships among major powers, affects the likelihood and process of reunification, as it affected the origin and process of division. The second is the way in which reunification itself changes the regional political landscape through its process and consequences. In reality, of course, the two are closely interlinked in reciprocal and dynamic ways. Disentangling this complex linkage is the purpose of this work.

Emerging Security Order: Implications for Reunification

In a paper presented at an international conference in Seoul, Kenneth Waltz warned against the *perils* of unbalanced power of the United

States in the post–Cold War world.[5] According to Waltz, the world is now characterized by its unipolar structure, with the United States as the only pole. Of the many configurations of international system structure including bipolar and multipolar ones, he contends that a unipolar one is the least stable, for two reasons. The first is the presence of a preponderant power, which threatens others by its very nature regardless of its intentions, and thereby elicits reactions such as arms buildups, alliance formations, and even wars, in attempts to balance it.[6] The second destabilizing effect of a unipolar system is the policy of the hegemonic state, which tends to be capricious and often threatening due to the absence of balancing power and action. According to Waltz, the United States in the post–Cold War era has been trapped by both of these perils.

An example that Waltz lists is the expansion of the North Atlantic Treaty Organization (NATO), which has weak reasons and strong ones against it. Among the many reasons against it is that "it pushes Russia toward China instead of drawing Russia toward Europe and America."[7] In my view, its Asian counterpart, which pushes China to reciprocate Russia's approach, is the United States–Japan Joint Declaration on Security made by President Clinton and Prime Minister Hashimoto in Tokyo in April 1996. Unlike the NATO expansion, however, the reasons for the new declaration may be as strong as the reasons against it. Still, the key point is that it may have triggered bifurcation of northeast Asian politics.

In fact, at the same time the joint declaration was made in Tokyo, President Yeltsin of Russia and President Jiang Zemin of China met in Beijing and declared an anti-hegemonism. A year later, when Hashimoto visited Washington, D.C., Jiang visited Moscow and issued a joint declaration of the Sino-Russian Strategic Partnership. In fact, the year 1997 witnessed a flurry of shuttle diplomacy at the summit level (see Table 1).

In addition to the April meetings just mentioned, the G-7 summit meetings were held in Denver in June. Hashimoto visited Beijing in September, with a return visit by Prime Minister Li Feng in November; and President Clinton invited Jiang to Washington, D.C., in September, at the same time that Hashimoto met Yeltsin in the Siberian city of Krasnoyarsk. In November, Yeltsin returned Jiang's visit to Moscow by visiting Beijing and reaffirming the Sino-Russian Strategic Partnership.

Considering the significance of some of these meetings, such as Jiang's visit to the United States, and the importance of the issues and depth of the discussions of others, like the Hashimoto–Yeltsin meeting in November, observers and analysts infer that the major powers are now actively searching for a new regional order, at least in East Asia, which has remained in flux and drew many speculations of future instability.[8] What will be the future political and security order in Northeast Asia? How will it alter the prospect and manner of Korean reunification?

Table 1. Summit Meetings of Four Major Powers in 1997

Who	*When*	*Where*	*What*
U.S.-Russia	March 20	Helsinki	Expansion of NATO, NATO-Russian Partnership
China-Russia	April 23	Moscow	Sino-Russian Strategic Partnership, Anti-Hegemonism
Japan-U.S.	April 25	Washington	Includes North Korean Policy Coordination
U.S.-Japan	June 19	Denver*	Includes the Korean Peninsula Issues
U.S.-Russia	June 21	Denver*	NATO Expansion, Russian Entrance to G-7
China-Japan	Sept. 5	Beijing	New U.S.-Japan Security Guideline; Security Cooperation
U.S.-China	Oct. 29	Washington	Search for Partnership; Human Rights; Trade Issues
Japan-Russia	Nov. 2	Krasnoyarsk	Peace Treaty by 2000; Northern Territories; Economic Cooperation
China-Russia	Nov. 10	Beijing	Agreement on Eastern Border; Reaffirmed Strategic Partnership
China-Japan	Nov. 12	Tokyo	Security Dialogue

* G-7 Summit Conference in Denver, Colorado, U.S.A.

Without digging deeply into the details of each power's policies and strategies, and accepting Waltz's prediction that the United States' unipolarity will not last, international theorists may easily posit three hypothetical forms of regional order based on history and/or theory: a neo-bipolar system, a "balance of power" system, and a concert of great powers system. A bipolar system here focuses more on alliance aggregation than on the number of great powers, and it could be either "loose" or "tight," depending on the strength of the alliance.[9] As alliance commitments get looser and the distribution of capabilities among major actors becomes more even, the system may turn to a balance-of-power system. Or, as major actors with comparable capabilities agree upon maintenance of the status quo, as European powers did after the Napoleonic War through the Concert of Europe, the system may properly be called a concert of great powers.

Could the apparent bifurcation of the East Asian major power system into the new United States–Japan security cooperation and the Sino-Russian strategic partnership become locked in such a spiral of mutual threat and distrust as to result in a new round of Cold War–like confrontation? Or is it simply a temporary alignment based on expediency, an expression of classic balance-of-power politics? Or, would the powers ever be able to realize their interdependence and come together with mutual understanding and interest in maintaining the status quo?

Bipolar aggregation of alliances in a multipolar Asia could be deadly, like the one in Europe before World War I has shown. Alliances in such a structure tend to be rigid and entangling, as allies are valued more than in a structurally bipolar system. In the latter, the pole states command more freedom from their smaller allies, not only because allies matter less but also because of bigger discrepancies in power between the patron and client states.[10] As conflicts of interest grow larger and animosity deeper between the poles, alliances tend to grow larger and larger as the powers in each pole competitively seek allies elsewhere and the lesser powers in the system begin to take sides.

The parallel of the new U.S.–Japan security cooperation and the Sino-Russian strategic partnership is particularly striking if one recalls what happened in the early 1970s. Despite the fact that the Americans had fought an extensive war with the Chinese in the Korean War of 1950–53, the United States invited China to the United Nations to replace Taiwan as a permanent member of the Security Council and normalized its relationship with China in order to play a China card against the Soviet Union. With the Cold War ended and the Soviet threat over, "containment" of China is now being actively discussed.[11] The U.S.–Japan alliance was rejuvenated when the threats it originally aimed against had disappeared. From a long-term perspective, then, one may be reminded of classic balance-of-power politics in East Asia. Nations in such a system try to balance power, i.e., to prevent any one nation from becoming preponderant through unilateral armaments, alliances, or compensations, and attempting to divide and rule.[12]

In the short term, however, the balance-of-power dynamics may be reduced to a concert of great powers, if temporarily, which realize how precarious the politico-military relationships are and how indispensable the economic ones are. In this situation, major powers agree that they cannot afford a major war or a Cold War, and put aside their differences for the sake of "peace and stability." After the Napoleonic War, European powers formed the Concert of Europe with a shared stake in restoring and maintaining the *status quo ante bellum* and avoiding major war among themselves. It might have been a rare example of a security regime,[13] but it was maintained only by the sacrifices of lesser powers, involving the division of Poland and interventions in the internal affairs of such lesser powers as Italy and Spain.

Before we assess the form of regional order most likely to emerge, let us examine how each order would influence Korean reunification. Located squarely in the middle of the strategic quadrangle, Korea has been strongly subject to and influenced by the fluctuations in this area of power politics. Each of the major powers has had great stakes in the Korean Peninsula and often fought wars with each other, as China and Japan did in 1894–95 and Russia and Japan did in 1904–05. Alternatively, the great powers would sometimes make agreements on their spheres of influence, as the United States and Japan did in 1905 with the Taft-Katsura agreement, and the United States and Russia did in 1945 in dividing the Korean Peninsula at the 38th parallel. Intervention by the

U.S.–led coalition and counter-intervention by China during the Korean War illustrate the geostrategic significance of Korea all too well.[14]

None of the three aforementioned systems of power facilitates Korean reunification. Instead, to a greater or lesser extent, each affects the prospect of reunification profoundly but negatively. First, if mutual distrust and antagonism between the United States and China are deeply embedded in the minds of the public and political leaders in each state, and if the Russian perceptions of threat from the United States and the Japanese perception of threat from the growing power of China are severe enough to push them to tightly align with China and the United States respectively, the emergence of a bipolar configuration is not entirely out of the question. Once adversarial relations between the two blocs are established, lesser powers surrounding them would be forced or tempted to take sides. Obviously, the divided Koreas will be the first ones to do so by allying themselves with opposing poles, and the Cold War politics in the peninsula would resume. Given that South Korea is firmly allied with the United States, and Japan is newly committed to aid the United States in any contingencies in Korea, South Korea would have to forgo the fruits of its successful Northern diplomacy, and North Korea's isolation would end.

Second, if the conflict of ideologies is over for good, and each of the great powers tries to increase its capabilities, either to become predominant or to balance any emerging power in a classic balance-of-power system, Korea may again become the pawn in the games they play. A worst-case scenario, typical balance-of-power politics, is that any of the immediately neighboring powers—namely China and Japan—may try to keep Korea divided lest the reunified and stronger Korea should become a threat.[15] A more probable scenario may be that either Japan or the United States would try to expand its influence to the desperately needy North Korea without regard to the issue of reunification. Or, Russia and/or China would try to keep the North under their respective influence. As will be discussed in the following section, if such efforts involve lucrative options and offers, Pyongyang would not come to any negotiating table with Seoul.

Third, major powers, concerned about the fragility of the relationships among themselves, may come to an agreement to maintain the status quo or "peace and stability" in the region even at the expense of their short-term, less-valued interests. Or, they may in fact have agreed to do so, an observer susceptible to conspiracy theories may guess. The biggest potential source of instability in the region is the Korean Peninsula, either in the form of North Korea's collapse in the short run or reunification in the longer run.[16] No power would be eager to save the failing North Korea, but more would protest—and each would welcome it if any of the others do. It may be China or Japan who salvages Pyongyang from collapsing. Again, Pyongyang would refuse to come to the negotiating table with Seoul.

A regional order that is the most congenial to Korean reunification will be a multilateral system of cooperative security, with many features of what Karl Deutsch calls the pluralistic security community.[17] In such a system, all the members, including the great powers, share a stake in avoiding war and maintaining peace and stability in the system. Yet they do not stop at simply managing the status quo. Instead, by actively searching and developing confidence-building measures, they strive to solve potential sources of conflict and keep any conflict from escalating because of mutual threat and fear. Any potential source of conflict is not just managed but a peaceful solution is sought from the beginning. In this system, Korean reunification would be welcome by system members as the fundamental resolution of one of the region's biggest sources of conflict. Furthermore, the system members would try to manage the process collectively and peacefully.

Korean Reunification Scenarios: Previous Studies

Korean reunification may be a fantasy to some people and a specter to some others, but its prospect is certainly higher than ever. The Cold War is over and Kim Il Sung is dead. North Korea is isolated and weakened, while the South Korean economy has recorded impressive growth. The gap between the two competing economies was as much as 22:1 in terms of gross national product (GNP) ratio and 12:1 in per capita GNP ratio in 1996 and is still widening rapidly.[18] The North Korean economy has continually recorded negative growth each year since 1990, when the Council on Mutual Economic Assistance (CMEA) was dissolved. Its entire population is suffering from a severe lack of food, mainly due to bad crops caused by heavy rains and flooding in 1995 and 1996.

Whereas South Korea celebrated a record harvest in many years in 1997, North Korea experienced another year of bad crops and food shortage.[19] The report was written by a reporter accompanying Congressman Tony Hall (D-Ohio) who was cited as saying that the food shortage had worsened significantly from what he saw during his visit last April. The reporter, who has also written on famines elsewhere, including Somalia, concluded that the Korean food shortage was not just the result of bad crops due to floods, nor even due to the ill-fated policy of *Juche* agriculture, but was an inescapable result of the entire North Korean system, which had ceased to function.[20]

Nevertheless, the reporter saw no sign of either mass revolt from below or reform from the top. This observation is echoed by many analyses, including one on the possibility and directions of change in North Korea.[21] The analysis lists three critical variables that will determine future courses of change in North Korea:

- the degree and extent of social discontent, and the ways in which the discontent gets expressed;
- the amount of conflict among the power elite and the stability of the current regime; and
- the external environment.

Depending upon various configurations and combinations of the variables, four scenarios are suggested:

- minimal change of the status quo;
- comprehensive reform efforts by a new, reform-oriented leadership;
- implosive collapse; and
- explosive collapse.

After analyzing these variables, the study concludes that the first scenario is the most likely because social discontent will not be organized in the North as no civil society has developed:

- no alternative leadership is on the horizon; and
- no drastic change in U.S. and Chinese policy toward Pyongyang is expected. The scenario involving minimal change will culminate in the eventual collapse of the system and its absorption by the South, the study further concludes.

Another major study, organized by the Samsung Economic Research Institute, was undertaken and published around the same time as the one just mentioned.[22] After a series of intensive workshops involving dozens of experts on North Korea and using the SRI (Stanford Research Institute) method, the study constructs four possible scenarios of reunification. The four scenarios are shown in Table 2, a two-by-two table with two critical variables: (1) U.S. and South Korean policy toward North Korea, and (2) the strength and policy orientation of political leadership in North Korea—measured in dichotomy.

Table 2. Types and Scenarios of Reunification: The Samsung Study

		North Korean Leadership	
		Soft-Weak	Hard-Strong
U.S. and South Korean	Support	*Inducement*	*Agreement*
Policy toward North Korea	Containment	*Self-destruction*	*Collision*

Reunification by agreement occurs when the U.S. and South Korean governments employ a supportive or engagement policy toward the North, and North Korean leadership is strong enough to successfully lead the society into reform and economic recovery without experiencing any destabilization. As North Korea continues to grow, balance of power will be restored between the two Koreas. After a rather lengthy period of peaceful coexistence, the two governments may reach an agreement to reunify on an equal basis.

Reunification by inducement occurs when the U.S. and South Korean governments employ a support or engagement policy toward the North and North Korean leadership is weak and soft. The support policy of the United States and South Korea will be followed by North Korean reform efforts. Being weak, however, reform efforts fail to recover the economy and meet rising public expectations. North Korea will be "induced" to reunify with South Korea on the latter's terms.

Reunification by self-destruction results when the U.S. and South Korean governments employ a containment policy toward the North and North Korean leadership is too weak to cope with the domestic instability caused by the economic hardship aggravated by the containment policy of the United States and South Korea. This leads to the collapse of the North Korean regime and state, and thereby to reunification through absorption by the South.

Reunification by collision results when the U.S. and South Korean governments employ a containment policy toward the North and North Korean leadership is strong and hawkish. The tensions in the Korean Peninsula escalate due to the U.S. and South Korean containment policy and North Korea's brinkmanship. Belligerent words from North Korea may beget belligerent deeds. War breaks out when North Korea launches a surprise attack or invites a U.S. and South Korean preemptive strike, or by escalation of small-scale border disputes. North Korea will lose, and reunification will ensue on Seoul's terms.[23]

This study has important limitations in two respects. The first, relatively minor to the second but still serious, is that it confounds two dimensions of the second critical variable, the strength and policy orientation of the North Korean leadership. Being hard or soft in policy orientation and strong or weak in leadership are totally different things. A strong leadership may take soft-line policies and weak leadership may still take hard-line policies. Or, considering the current policy lines of North Korea, a strong leadership can shift to soft-line policy because it is strong, and a weak leadership may have to stay with a hard-line policy because it is unable to change the course of action.

The second limitation is common to both of the studies just discussed and is more severe and potentially fatal. Both analyses generally ignore the role of neighboring powers, which can prove decisive at critical junctures. For example, one of the main variables in the Samsung study is U.S. *and* South Korean policy toward the North, implicitly assuming that American and South Korean governments are in full agreement with respect to their policies toward the North. Is it a safe assumption?[24] Or, one of the three critical variables in the study by Seo is the international environment, but throughout his article, this variable is paid only passing attention and is conceptualized vaguely in terms of U.S. and Chinese policies toward the North.[*]

Reunification Scenarios and Emerging Regional Orders

Considering the international nature of the Korean issue, neglecting the role of neighboring powers is not only unwarranted but also even risky. In this section, I examine how the emerging regional orders discussed earlier affect and are affected by each reunification scenario. To do so, I first reconstruct the base-case scenarios of reunification with little regard for the roles of neighboring powers. The scenarios are largely based on the aforementioned studies, but other studies are also taken into consideration.[25]

Base-Case Reunification Scenarios

First, reunification by the collapse or implosion of the North Korean regime and/or state may be started by a mass revolt—perhaps triggered by a skirmish between the authorities and a group of people over the distribution of food[26] or subversive actions by South Korean agents—or by an armed power struggle within the ruling elite. In either case, massive outflows of refugees would pass through the northern border with China, through the West (Yellow) Sea and East Sea (of Japan), and perhaps even over the DMZ, as the result of the loosening or loss of control by the North Korean authority. A large number of casualties could result—North Korean border guards might fire on the refugees; many might get stranded in the open sea, in which case they could starve or drown before reaching the coasts of China, Japan, or South Korea or being picked up by passing ships; and some might be killed by land mines inside the DMZ. Foreign powers might be invited by one or more of the warring parties in the North, or sanctioned by an international authority like the United Nations, or tempted out of self-interest to intervene in the situation. The most peaceful, if not most likely, resolution of the situation would be for the North Korean authority, totally incapacitated, to turn to the South for help, or to the international community, which is willing and ready to help the South Korean government take over the North.

Second, reunification by collision or explosion will be the result of a war, initiated by Pyongyang out of desperation, miscalculation of the probability of winning, or escalated from a small skirmish in the DMZ—a calculated provocation by the North for certain political motives. The North can take advantage of surprise attack or *blitzkrieg* to cause extreme instability in South Korean society and achieve some initial successes in battle. But it will soon face heavy attacks by the high-tech weapons of the combined forces of the United States and South Korea with the war turning to a stalemate and then slowly to the defeat of the North. The war may briefly rally and mobilize North Korean society, but soon the starving people will begin to flee as food rationing stops altogether and the government loses control over the society, resulting in chaos. Even before the combined forces actually overrun the North in the battlefields, the North Korean system may collapse and the combined forces may take over the North militarily and politically.

Third, reunification by inducement can happen as the result of a comprehensive reform program launched by Pyongyang. After an unsuccessful trial of limited openness in Rajin-Sonbong special economic zones, the North Korean regime decides to speed its opening-up not only in scope but also in depth. Investments by South Korean businesses take the lead, followed by some Western investors. Pyongyang also allows private farming and ownership of lands to ease the food shortage. Such moves may record some initial successes, but the North Korean people become increasingly exposed to the outside world and especially to South Korea.[27] The people's expectations begin to exceed what the system can offer, and the calls for unconditional reunification soar. Unable to meet such expectations and under heavy pressure for reunification, which will be enthusiastically welcomed by the South, Pyongyang will have no choice but to negotiate with Seoul and agree to reunification on mostly South Korean terms. Or, as an increasing number of North Koreans see windows of opportunity in the South, they try to smuggle themselves into the South as many ethnic Koreans from Manchuria have done during the past six or seven years. The end result could parallel what happened in East Germany—absorption of the poorer Korea by the richer one.

Fourth and last, I do not believe that reunification by political agreement between the two Korean governments, envisaged in the Samsung study, is likely. In the short run, any political agreement between the two systems, which are nearly antithetical in every aspect and have developed such antagonism, is almost impossible.[28] Or, even if reunification by agreement happens, it will remain highly unstable, as happened in Yemen. In the longer run, on the other hand, any political agreement after North Korea successfully reforms and restores its economy and achieves parity with the South, as envisioned in the Samsung study, is hard to imagine. First, North Korean reform is not likely to succeed without being "induced" to reunify. Second, if North Korea ever succeeds in catching up with the South economically, it will have less incentive to reunify. With the huge gap in the level of economic development of the two Koreas—an 11.6:1 ratio in GNP per capita—catching up would take too long for any nationalistic identity and emotion for reunification to endure.[29]

A fourth scenario therefore assumes that the North Korean system is more durable than many think and predicts that it will stay with or "muddle through" the current policy and situation or the "march of hardship," a North Korean version of the "long march." As the study by Seo indicates, this would eventually lead to its collapse and absorption by the South. The only difference from the implosion scenario is that this would take longer and foreign powers would be more likely to intervene to save Pyongyang in the meantime.

Which of the scenarios is the most likely to happen? The Samsung study also conducted a survey that asked two groups of experts which scenario is the most likely to occur. One of the groups consisted of 55 people who are researchers, professors, journalists, and active and retired government officials with general interest in and knowledge about inter-Korean and reunification issues. The other group is in fact a subgroup of the former, consisting of twenty experts or specialists on the reunification issue in particular. Table 3 reports the results of the survey.[30]

The survey is not scientific and statistical inference is not its purpose. But reunification by inducement is the mostly likely to happen, while reunification by implosion is only slightly less likely. But it is troublesome that experts believe reunification by agreement is more likely than a collision-explosion scenario. Such a belief may merely reflect the wishful thinking of many South Koreans, who abhor the idea of war with a brother nation and generally prefer mutual "autonomous" reunification. In my view, the likelihood of collision or explosion could be as high

Table 3. Likelihood of Each Scenarios: The Samsung Study

	General Experts (%)		*Special Experts (%)*		*When to Happen?*
Agreement	8	(14.5)	1	(5.0)	after 20 years or more
Inducement	23	(41.8)	10	(50.0)	in 5-15 years
Self-Destruction	21	(38.2)	9	(45.0)	in 3-10 years
Collision	3	(5.5)	0	(0.0)	in 3-5 years
Number of Respondents	55		20		

as, or even higher than, that of political agreement to reunify.

Generally speaking, three out of four base scenarios—implosion, inducement, and muddling through—can be regarded as more or less equally probable, while the probability of explosion is somewhat less likely, but still probable. Such a rating of probabilities may seem arbitrary, but any other rating could be arbitrary as well. In the following sections, therefore, equi-probability serves as a null state against which the role of foreign powers is evaluated.

Neo-Bipolar System

In a neo-bipolar system, the probability of reunification by collision or by explosion of North Korea will increase, but the likelihood of reunification as a result of war will decrease. North Korean leadership will be strengthened and their policy stance hardened as China and Russia support them politically, militarily, and economically. Naturally, U.S. and South Korean policy will turn toward a policy of containment. Even if they choose an engagement policy, Pyongyang will not reciprocate. Thus, reunification by inducement or by agreement is generally out of the question.

The likelihood of immediate collapse or implosion will sharply decrease, owing to support by China and Russia. Overall, therefore, the probability of muddling through, with a possibility of eventual collapse, will be the most likely of all the scenarios. Economic support from China and Russia will remain minimal or marginal, and simple material input will not save the North Korean economy. Rather, it is more likely that China and Russia themselves will be in economic trouble due to weakened ties with the United States and Japan.

It is possible, and indeed likely, in this kind of system that China, under severe pressure from its population growth and rising expectations, may bolster North Korea's adventurism. If North Korea ever attacks the South out of bravado or desperation, the result could be devastating. For it cannot be ruled out that while the United States would get involved because of treaty obligation, and particularly by virtue of the U.S. forces in Korea, either China or Russia or both might support Pyongyang, through direct or indirect means. A North-South Korean war could be bigger in scope, longer in duration, and end up short of total victory and reunification.

Alternatively, if North Korea were to collapse due to its internal and endogenous developments and regardless of, or in spite of, the support from China and/or Russia, it is quite possible that either or both of them would belatedly intervene in the situation to save their valued ally. In this case, they would collide with U.S. and Japanese efforts to support their South Korean ally in taking control of North Korea.

Balance-of-Power System

In a regional situation of classical balance-of-power politics, it is likely that either or both the United States and Japan would seek to expand their spheres of influence into North Korea, assuming that South Korea is firmly under their influence. If the United States hastens its rapprochement with North Korea, Japan will try to neutralize or balance American ascendance by a countervailing approach to the North, perhaps in the name of normalizing relationships and including a lucrative offer of up to ten billion U.S. dollars in reparation. Such moves could create political tensions between the United States and Japan on the one hand and South Korea on the other, and precipitate a closer alignment between China and South Korea. Alternatively, China and/or Russia may try to counter such moves by their own offers to North Korea, smaller in amount but perhaps as effective as the American and Japanese offers, because of their traditional ties.

In such a happy situation, Pyongyang will refuse to talk to Seoul more stubbornly than ever and might be able to muddle through for some time before it finally faces collapse. It is still possible that the market economy may be an integrating force once Pyongyang, bolstered by its favorable position, launches a reform program and the South Korean economy, either directly or indirectly, gets involved. Therefore, reunification by inducement is not out of the question.

The probability of explosion will become lower as Pyongyang becomes less desperate and is discouraged by all its neighboring powers. If it ever happens, however, it may elicit intervention by all four powers, as the situation dictates. Or if North Korea implodes, particularly because of an internal armed power struggle, it is still possible that all of the powers would intervene in the situation directly or indirectly. In both cases, the end result could be highly disastrous in terms of regional stability and peace. From a short-term perspective, however, it is most likely that North Korea will muddle through and that Korea will remain divided and continue to be a major source of instability for a considerable period.

Concert of Great Powers

The great powers are beset by many sources of conflict, and they are each aware of the fact. They want to resolve them through peaceful means because none of them can afford large-scale war or even a cold war. They agree that they need time to find mutually acceptable solutions, and they manage the status quo to avoid catastrophe. Among the possible conflicts faced by the present concert of great powers, the Korean question may be regarded as potentially the most threatening. Any change in the status quo on the Korean Peninsula becomes worrisome.

If the two Koreas can agree on a political agenda to reunify, no reasonable rationale or substantive interest will lead the great powers to act against the reunification. But the great powers have a shared stake in preventing any disruptive and potentially uncontrollable situation. Should such a situation occur, they will feel a strong need for coordinated action.

Under such a system, the probability of abrupt changes, including an implosion-collapse of North Korea and/or a North Korean explosion or armed attack would be significantly limited. Any initiative by one or more powers to keep the North from imploding or exploding would be agreed to by the rest of the powers, although there is high probability that each would try to "pass the buck."[31] However, once there is an apparent signal of such change, the powers may well call a conference to coordinate their actions. They will very likely agree to measures to restore the *status quo ante*, until events run out of control.

At that point, then, the probability of reunification by either implosion-collapse or explosion-aggression would be reduced significantly. It is likely that China would try to keep the North from collapsing through giving minimal aid, and that Japan would then come in to hasten its diplomatic normalization with the North and provide the reparation money that Pyongyang desperately needs. It is only in this system, a concert of great powers, that the United States should welcome or acquiesce in such initiatives by China or Japan. The potential danger of North Korea's explosion may be bought off by similar moves. For, in this system of the status quo, both implosion and explosion take on the same meaning: a major disruption of the status quo.

Notwithstanding such preventive measures, events could still get out of hand. If that happens, the great powers will try to reach an agreement on the cheapest and least disruptive solutions. They would likely reach an agreement to stand behind South Korean efforts to handle the situation. This could turn out to be a stepping stone toward a multilateral cooperative security regime. Overall, however, the probability of North Korea muddling through on its own is highest, with the long-term possibility of collapse or inducement.

Multilateral System of Cooperative Security

In the idealized form just described, this system is rather distant from the realities, although there have been embryonic moves such as the ASEAN regional forum (ARF), the opportunity for discussions at the Asia-Pacific Economic Cooperation (APEC) summits, and other two-track meetings. There remain at least as many sources of conflict as possibilities for cooperation among the major powers, between the major powers and the lesser powers, and among the lesser powers. They range from deep-seated historical animosities and differences in societal organization and national values to more temporal territorial and trade disputes.

Nevertheless, this vision of cooperation is receiving increasing respect, owing to a combination of factors. One is the surge of international organizations and institutions, globally and locally. International organizations with global scope bring about the diffusion of certain norms and rules prevailing in other regions, with powerful pacifying effects. The events in Western Europe cannot occur without affecting politics in East Asia. Another, and more important impetus, is the economic dynamism in the region and the ever-growing economic interdependence among its nations, from the Pacific Rim throughout Northeast Asia. Although the Asia-Pacific region is as diverse as any region in the world, with smaller countries that may be unable to move beyond their immediate concerns, it happens to comprise many great powers with a region-wide and even global range of interests.

It has often been the case that multilateral forums such as ARF and APEC have provided forums where differences rather than similarities of interest get exposed. But such forums are still valuable because they expose those differences to debate.[32] If regional countries share a commitment to mutually beneficial economic interdependence and peaceful resolution of conflicts, the principle of cooperative security can be the desired norm. When cooperative security prevails, a potential source of conflict should be resolved rather than managed through collective effort. If the perception arises that the division of the Korean Peninsula, coupled with the unpredictable situation and policies of North Korea, is a serious source of conflicts, collective efforts may ensue to resolve them permanently. In such a climate, reunification would be welcomed as the path to resolution. If cooperative support incurs certain costs to the countries concerned, there would be ample room for intensive bargaining, but it could still be negotiated.

The foremost merit of a multilateral system is its flexibility and stability in meeting a variety of contingencies, without losing its stability. Defined as "an institutional form that coordinates relations among three or more states on the basis of generalized principles of conduct,"[33] multilateralism enjoys two essential advantages over other forms of institutions. First, multilateral institutions facilitate cooperation among nations. This property stems from the fact that a multilateral setting opens new possibilities of quid pro quo that are unavailable in a bilateral setting—an expression of "diffuse reciprocity."[34] Further, cooperation begets cooperation as nations build longer-term perspectives and "the shadow of the future" looms large.[35] Second, multilateral institutions in general, enjoy greater stability than institutions based on "the particularistic interests of the parties or the strategic exigencies that may exist in any specific occurrence."[36] That is, multilateral institutions react to unexpected changes and contingencies more elastically than institutions with particularistic purposes.

Given that the Asia-Pacific region is riddled with a wide variety of sources of conflict, of which the extreme unpredictability in the Korean Peninsula is only one, a multilateral system of cooperative security will provide the best forum for handling the Korean issue. In this kind of system, the likelihood of abrupt changes in North Korea in the form of implosion and explosion remains real. But the probability that such changes will result in regionwide instability is significantly reduced. It is up to the North Korean leadership either to stay closed and try to muddle through, or to open up and reform their economy at the risk of absorption or inducement. But in this system, the maneuverable space of both North and South Korean governments is wider than in other systems.

Table 4. The Impacts of Different Types of Regional Order on Korean Reunification

	Scenarios of Korean Reunification (or Changes in North Korea)			
	Muddling Through	*Implosion/Collapse*	*Explosion/Collision*	*Inducement*
The Base Case Scenario	North Korea stays on the current course of policy, getting limited outside aids, tries limited reform and opening with little success, while keeping tight control over the society. It may muddle through the years of hardship for some time, but eventually collapses and absorbed by the South.	North Korea regime/state collapses and is absorbed by the South, following massive outflows of refugees region-wide, triggered by armed power struggle among the ruling elite and/or mass revolt escalated from small skirmish between people and the authority over the distribution of foods.	North Korea launches armed attack on the South either out of desperation or from miscalculated adventurism, only to result in military occupation by the U.S. and South Korean forces. North Korea may collapse due to the loss of control and social dislocation during wartime.	Unsuccessful or partially successful reform generates people's expectations that the system cannot meet. Increased contacts with South Korea raise the calls for reunification. Increasing number of people smuggle themselves into the South and Pyongyang accepts reunification on South Korean terms.
Neo-Bipolar System	North Korea will more likely choose this option and stay longer as China a/o Russia supports Pyongyang.	Probability sharply decreases, but largely as a matter of timing. North Korea will muddle through longer, but eventually collapse, as external supports will not restore the economy.	Probability increases as North Korean leadership is bolstered by external supports. But reunification as the end result is not likely.	Probability sharply decreases, as North Korean leadership will opt for muddling through.
Classic Balance-of-Power System	Probability drastically increases as major powers competitively support Pyongyang. North Korea will be able to stay longer than in any other system.	Probability drastically decreases, but if this ever happens, it will destabilize the region greatly.	Probability decreases somewhat, but if this ever happens, it could be devastating to the regional stability.	Probability decreases. Pyongyang, encouraged by favorable int'l environment, may opt for reform, but reunification may not ensue as Pyongyang turns to major powers before Seoul.
Concert of Great Powers	Probability increases greatly as North Korea will be able to get emergency helps whenever necessary. Still such temporary helps will not be enough to save it.	Probabilities of abrupt changes like this decrease with the first aid support from outside. But its destructive potential grows like cancer cells.	Probability decreases as major powers may try to buy off such options from Pyongyang. Chance of crisis remains high as Pyongyang employs brinkmanship to gain more.	Probability will decrease as Pyongyang regards muddling through as a more viable option.
Multilateral System of Cooperative Security	Probability remains about the same as the base scenario, but slowly goes down as Pyongyang finds increasing incentives in reforms and opening.	In short run, probability remains high but the process will be handled peacefully and effectively through joint efforts by the nations concerned. Over the long run, probability will go down as Pyongyang opts for reform.	Probability will go down, as escalation becomes less likely. Through concerted efforts by nations concerned and the logic of defensive cooperation, Pyongyang may be induced to be a member of the system eventually.	Probability will generally go up and go even higher, if Pyongyang is induced to take part in the system, and then encouraged to take comprehensive reform of its system.

Table 5. The Impacts of Different Types and Scenarios of Reunification on Future of Regional Order

	Types of Regional Order in Northeast Asia			
	Neo-Bipolar System	*Balance-of-Power System*	*Concert of Great Powers*	*Multilateral System of Coop. Security*
The Base Case Scenario	The U.S.-China relation deteriorates as the U.S. tightens its charge against human rights abuse in China. The U.S. and Japan step up their security cooperation in terms of joint military exercises. China and Russia get ever closer with China's shopping spree of Russian arms.	The relationships among major powers remain tense. The U.S. and Japan normalizes diplomatic relations with Pyongyang, while China a/o Russia offer new treaty of mutual assistance to Pyongyang. Seoul builds up armament with purchase from Russia, and Japan speeds up its military modernization.	Major powers develop mutual understanding and interests in the status quo. Whenever there is a sign of abrupt events, they collectively intervene or authorize one of them to intervene in the situation to restore the status quo.	China agrees to some arms control measures, begins to scale down its military and U.S. manages its military presence in less threatening manner. Russia controls its arms transfer quid pro quo economic cooperation from Japan. Pyongyang reluctantly joins in the system and begins arms control talks with Seoul.
Muddling Through	China a/o Russia become increasingly suspicious of U.S. a/o Japanese intentions approaching Pyongyang, reluctant to cooperate with the U.S. on the Korean question, and steps up their support of Pyongyang by reaffirming their security commitments.	U.S. experiences difficulties in the missile talks with Pyongyang, pressures the latter harder, and meets Chinese oppositions. The U.S.-China relation deteriorates and the system turns to a neo-polar system.	Pyongyang keeps its brinkmanship diplomacy to get more aids from major powers, inter-Korean relations get worse and the Peninsula remain highly unstable. Still major powers are unable to resolve the situation fundamentally.	Pyongyang finds itself under increasing pressure to reform, slowly and cautiously starts it. Then Pyongyang speeds it up as it finds reform not so destabilizing than it thinks. Hawkish opinion in Seoul is silenced.
Implosion/ Collapse	U.S.-China relation rapidly worsens as the U.S. leads international interventions in North Korea and China vehemently opposes interventions in "domestic affairs."	Negotiations for possible joint intervention fail; powers competitively intervene by supporting opposing parties; and blame each other for protraction of the bloody situation.	Major powers agree at joint intervention but fail to act. Countries affected the most act alone, blame others for non-action. The Concert breaks down.	Regional countries huddle to discuss joint actions. Collective intervention under the auspices of US a/o regional organization is agreed upon.
Explosion/ Collision	China vetoes any UN actions. The U.S. bombards Pyongyang with utmost firepower. China gathers its troops in Manchuria, warns against U.S. marching North of the 38th Parallel, and calls for cease-fire.	The situation is similar to neo-bipolar system. Yet, Japan plays more active and independent roles, perhaps the role of a mediator, despite vehement objections by Seoul.	The U.S. intervenes, but stops at restoring the status quo ante, and agrees to early cease-fire despite Seoul's objection. Implosion of North Korea will ensue.	Escalation of accident violence is prevented. Unprovoked aggression meets firm and resolute collective resistance. Regional countries support the U.S.-South Korean efforts to reunify.
Inducement	Not likely, but if it happens, it will follow the path of implosion, as Pyongyang closes down the society instead of turning the power to Seoul.	Unlikely as Pyongyang will turn to major powers for help before it does to Seoul. If major powers fail to act, implosion may ensue.	Unlikely, but if it happens in a peaceful way, major powers will not intervene.	Regional countries welcome the moves and discuss the ways to support Seoul's efforts to reconstruct North Korean economy.

The discussions so far in this section are summarized in Tables 4 and 5. Table 4 discusses how different configurations of regional order, listed in rows, can influence the probability, timing, and potential costs of each reunification scenario, shown in columns. Conversely, Table 5 illustrates how reunification in each scenario, shown in rows, affects regional orders. Table 5 in particular provides illustrations, rather than general discussion, but it demonstrates an important point: that the process of reunification can affect the shaping of the regional order if it is still in flux, or transform the order if it is still unstable.

Policy Implications and Proposals

The discussion so far can yield important policy implications for the governments of the major powers, as well as for South Korea and North Korea. But to discuss policy implications and proposals, one needs to consider the interests of the actors concerned, the options they have, and the constraints they face.

South Korean interests lie in the *earliest achievement of peaceful reunification with the least cost to its own terms*, although the values involved may be in a trade-off relationship. For instance, the dispute over whether earlier reunification is preferable to a less costly one is particularly acute. A general consensus, hence, the official policy of the government, is similar to reunification by "inducement," although the policy does not explicitly name absorption as the possible result of inducement.

The options for the South Korean government are limited, however. It continued to call for a bilateral dialogue between North and South Korea, which Pyongyang refuses, particularly since the death of Kim Il Sung in the summer of 1994. Pyongyang has not honored the basic agreement of February 1992, or the Agreement on Reconciliation, Nonaggression, and Exchanges and Cooperation, particularly the plan to begin exchanges. No significant interactions between the two societies have occurred other than the ones involving the light water reactor (LWR) project. Seoul hopes that Pyongyang is ready to engage in inter-Korean economic exchanges and that it will reform its system and open its society. But the more Seoul wants it, the more suspicious Pyongyang becomes of Seoul's intentions, and the more concerned about the political consequences.

Seoul's options are limited because it faces many constraints, perhaps far more than foreign governments realize. For years, the South Korean people have worried about the *costs* of reunification. The German experience is often invoked and compared to the Korean case. The most common worry is that the North Korean economy is far worse than East Germany's was, and for South Korea, with fewer resources than West Germany, the reunification costs would be unbearable. A more important source of constraint lies in the domestic society and people's attitudes. South Koreans hold a dual image of North Korea: a brother nation on the one hand and an archenemy on the other. Policies that look too hawkish or tough on the "brother" are not welcome, while policies that are too soft on the "enemy" are equally unwelcome.[37] The range of policy options is thus severely limited.

North Korean interests mostly mirror those of the South. Pyongyang certainly wants reunification on its own terms as early as possible. And it would, without doubt, prefer peaceful reunification or reunification by subverting the South Korean government/state rather than by an outright war, although it has not ruled out the latter option.

North Korea, however, has found its range of options rapidly shrinking. Its economy is failing and people are starving. Morale can only be low, and fuel to run military equipment is lacking. To recover its economy would mean restructuring its system, particularly the economic system, and opening it to foreign investments. Yet, restructuring and opening up obviously risks the viability of the system, particularly in the face of an omnivorous South Korean economy. The leadership of Kim Jung Il may be strong, but not strong enough to change the policy course set by his father, on whose authority the leadership still heavily depends. The only resource it could mobilize is military muscle, and wielding it has jeopardized its program of luring foreign investments into the special economic zones.

The long-term interests of the United States lie in reunification of the Korean Peninsula on the terms of its South Korean ally, in a peaceful manner. Yet its short-term interests lie in preventing any crisis in the peninsula, for this would greatly destabilize the region, and most of all, entangle the United States directly in the crisis, risking thousands of American lives and billions or trillions of dollars.

These short-term interests are shared by other regional powers, particularly China, who believes any crisis and potentially destabilizing conflict would prove extremely detrimental to its priority program of economic modernization. Such events would jeopardize China's economic development, not only by their immediate impact on its economic activities, but also by their broad political consequences. That is why Beijing agreed to participate in the four-party talks. Concern for the region's stability has also made other regional powers, such as Japan and Russia, welcome the four-party talks, although they may prefer to play more active roles.

China's long-term interests may differ from those of the United States, however. Obviously, China would prefer the divided Korea to one reunified solely on South Korean terms. I do not subscribe to the conspiracy theory that suggests that Japan secretly desires the permanent division of the Korean Peninsula, but the possibility is nevertheless considered in Tables 4 and 5.

Korean reunification could still come, regardless of the desires, hidden or open, of other nations. From the perspective of the Korean people, reunification should come for reasons of nationalistic zeal, the normative imperative for peace, and the promise of substantive dividends. Thus, the common interests of all the regional countries should be reunification of the Korean Peninsula in the least destabilizing fashion.

Many expected that North Korea would come to the negotiating table with the South not only because of the four-party talks, but also for bilateral North-South dialogues in connection with the inauguration of the Kim Dae Jung presidency in the South. There were two reasons for this. First, North Korea would demonstrate its genuine interest in peace and stability in the Korean Peninsula in order to lure the foreign investments it so badly needs. And second, Pyongyang would have exhausted its rationale for refusing a dialogue with Seoul after the inauguration of a new president in the South. For Pyongyang refused to talk to President Kim Young Sam, whom Pyongyang accused of having tarnished the name of its great leader after his death.

Of course, it is very likely that North Korean participation in the four-party talks or North-South dialogue has only a tactical purpose, without sincere interest in improving inter-Korean relations, or especially, inter-Korean exchanges. The aborted four-party talks in Geneva in December 1997 and a bilateral talk in Beijing in April 1998 lend support to this suspicion. Still, any dialogue will provide a thread Seoul could and should hang on to for improving the prospect of peaceful reunification.

When the opportunity presents itself, the South Korean government should try to build a substantive and constructive relationship between the two Koreas. Substantive means that any development in the inter-Korean relationship should involve not just a declaration of political will, but an irreversible commitment of resources. The history of inter-Korean dialogue during the past two and one-half decades, including the most recent case of the Basic Agreement of 1992, has shown that "getting over the mutual distrust and building confidence between the two Koreas through dialogue is like Sisyphus pushing the stone over the hill, which is only to roll down to the bottom of the valley even by a smallest agitation."[37] Instead of repeating such experiences, any new exchange between the two Koreas should pave a way that, even if the current exchange stalls, ensures they do not have to start from scratch.

Taking a constructive path means that any improvement in inter-Korean relations should aim to give both parties practical gains, so that cooperation begets cooperation and develops its own momentum. Therefore, the future development of an inter-Korean relationship should involve exchanges and cooperation at the practical level, rather than any declaration of, or agreement on, the principles of reunification. In particular, the South Korean government should resist the temptation to link any political motives to exchanges and cooperation at the practical level, for this would backfire soon after an allergic Pyongyang suspected it.

In light of the foregoing discussion, what the regional countries need is to develop some form of multilateral institutions of regional security. To be multilateral means that the basic principles of such institutions must be generalized. The institutions need not and should not aim at the particular Korean question. Instead, they need to address the general issue of regional security in terms of common and cooperative security.

When the South Korean government proposed a Northeast Asian Security Dialogue (NEASED) of six nations, namely China, Japan, Russia, the United States, and the two Koreas, at the inaugural meeting of ARF and kept proposing it until 1996, it was not welcomed with enthusiasm by any of the proposed members.

The proposal was unfortunately misconceived in that its intent was to deal mainly with the Korean issue, even if not explicitly stated. This motive was revealed by the fact that North Korea was not a member of ARF, and the proposal was not repeated at the 1997 meeting, as the four-party talks proposal was put forward. Any multilateral institution with a particularistic purpose would not work out in practice because, for instance, it would give North Korea a veto power at its inception. In contrast, a six-party dialogue for the purpose of broader regional security could still be productive. A more practical formula would be a security dialogue of five parties in the context of ARF until North Korea joins it.[38] Multilateral institutions tend to induce reluctant outsiders to join and "cooperate defensively," for remaining outside would hurt them more than coming in.[39]

When such a forum gets its own momentum and nations find it serving their interests, it could function effectively to meet many contingencies in regional security issues. North Korea, believing that economic reform and opening up are imperative, may find that taking such a policy course may not be as dangerous as it initially believed. Or, eventually, Pyongyang may come to the conclusion that economic reform and opening are the only options they can possibly choose in order to save its failing economy and, most of all, its starving people, even at the risk of induced reunification. Even if that happens, Pyongyang may try to impose as many of its own terms of reunification as possible.

Conclusion

So far in this paper, I have discussed how the process of Korean reunification and the future of East Asian security are interrelated. Specifically, it was argued that while the nature of the next regional security order would profoundly shape the likelihood and process of reunification, the form and stability of the future order would also be determined to a great extent by how reunification unfolds. Therefore, political leaders of concerned countries need to maintain a broader and longer-term perspective when they address the Korean issues. That is, while the region needs a new security order to fit the new realities brought about by the end of the Cold War, the new order needs to be highly elastic to cope with many contingencies that could arise from the reunification process.

Because of the economic crisis that has swept many East Asian countries since the summer of 1997, the Korean issue has received relatively little attention.[40] But precisely because of the uncertainties and anxieties of the economic crisis, any exigencies that arise in North Korea could be far more destabilizing than they might be otherwise. It is hoped that the arguments in this chapter, although often inconclusive, will prompt widespread discussion and deep analyses of the issues so that people can better understand them and that policy makers can propose more prudent policy measures.

Notes

[1] See Sean Lynn-Jones and Steven Miller, eds., *The Cold War and After: Prospects for Peace*, expanded edition (Cambridge, Mass.: The MIT Press, 1994), especially John J. Mearsheimer, "Back to the Future: Instability in Europe After the Cold War," and Stephen Van Evera, "Primed for Peace: Europe After the Cold War," for pessimistic and optimistic appraisal of future European security, respectively.

[2] See Jack Snyder, "Averting Anarchy in the New Europe," in *The Cold War and After.*

[3] See Taehyun Kim, "Globalization and Modernization, and East Asia at a Crossroads: A Perspective on East Asian Security Order," *Korea and World Affairs*, Vol. 21, No. 1 (Spring 1997) for a general discussion of stabilizing and destabilizing elements for East Asian security.

[4] Van Evara, "Primed for Peace"; Aaron Friedberg, "Ripe for Rivalry: Prospects for Peace in a Multipolar Asia," in Michael E. Brown, Sean M. Lynn-Jones, and Steven E. Miller, eds., *East Asian Security: An International Security Reader* (Cambridge, Mass.: The MIT Press, 1996).

[5] Kenneth N. Waltz, "The Changing Global Balance." Paper presented at the International Conference on "Visions and Realities in the 21st Century: The Role of East Asia," organized by the Graduate School of Peace Studies, Kyung Hee University, Seoul, Korea, September 1997.

[6] Recall Thucydides's dictum that "the real, but unavowed cause [of the Peloponnesian War] I consider to have been the growth of the power of Athens, and the alarm which it inspired in Lacadaemon; this made war inevitable," although Athens protested that "circumstances first compelled us to develop our empire to its present size, fear was our principal motive." Thucydides, *The History of the Peloponnesian War*, edited in translation by Sir Richard Livingston (London: Oxford University Press, 1943), pp. 46, 61.

[7] Waltz, "The Changing Global Balance," p. 4.

[8] See collection of articles in Brown, et al., eds., *East Asian Security.*

[9] Cf., see Morton A. Kaplan, *System and Process in International Politics* (New York: John Wiley, 1957), ch. 2.

[10] Kenneth N. Waltz, *Theory of International Politics* (Reading, MA: Addison-Wesley, 1979).

[11] See, e.g., Richard Bernstein and Ross H. Munro, *The Coming Conflict with China* (New York: Knopf, 1997).

[12] Waltz, *Theory of International Politics*; Hans J. Morgenthau, *Politics Among Nations: The Struggle for Power and Peace*, 5th edition (New York: Alfred Knopf, 1973), pp. 178ff.

[13] Robert Jervis, "Security Regimes," in Stephen D. Krasner, ed., *International Regimes* (Ithaca, NY: Cornell University Press, 1983).

[14] Although he misunderstands part of the history, Morgenthau discusses the Korean issue in the same vein in *Politics Among Nations*, p. 177.

[15] Ibid., p. 178.

[16] In this case, the potential for instability in the Taiwan straits would be lower than it is in the Korean Peninsula because China, agreeing to the status quo, would not push Taiwan hard enough to offend other powers and the others would not support any movement by Taiwan toward independence.

[17] Karl W. Deutsch, et al., *Political Community and the North Atlantic Area* (Princeton, N.J.: Princeton University Press, 1957). For the concept of cooperative security and its application to the Asia-Pacific region, see Janne E. Nolan, ed., *Global Engagement: Cooperation and Security in the 21st Century* (Washington, D.C.: The Brookings Institution, 1994), ch. 1 and ch. 11, Harry Harding, "Cooperative Security in the Asia-Pacific Region." For the nature and merits of multilateralism, see John

G. Ruggie, *Multilateralism Matters: The Theory and Praxis of an Institutional Form* (New York: Columbia University Press, 1993).

[18] The ratio of GNP was 11:1 in 1990. The Bank of Korea, "Estimation of North Korean Economy, 1996," cited in *Hankuk Kyongje Shinmun* (*Korea Economic Daily*), July 10, 1997.

[19] Keith B. Richburg, "North Korea on Brink of New Crisis," *Washington Post*, Oct. 18, 1997.

[20] Keith B. Richburg, "Beyond a Wall of Secrecy: Devastation," *Washington Post*, Oct. 19, 1997.

[21] Jin-Young Seo, "Crisis of the North Korean System and Four Scenarios of Change," *Chongchaek Nondan* [Policy Forum], Vol. 3, No. 2 (1996) (in Korean).

[22] Jong-Suh Ku, et al., *Korean Reunification Scenarios* (Seoul: Samsung Economic Research Institute, Oct. 1996), p. 21 (in Korean).

[23] Ibid., pp. 20–21.

[24] There have been an increasing number of reports of the tension between Washington and Seoul, particularly over North Korean policy. See Nicholas D. Kristof, "How a Stalled Submarine Sank North Korea's Hope," *New York Times*, November 17, 1996; Anthony Spaeth, "Amity Runs Aground," *Time*, Oct. 28, 1996; R. Jeffrey Smith, "United States Aides Pessimistic on Korean Talks," *Washington Post*, Oct. 13, 1997.

*See "footnote 26"

[25] Those others include Seo, "Crisis of the North Korean System"; Ho-Min Yang, et al., *North and South Korea: The Road to Reunification* (Seoul: Nanam, 1992) (in Korean); Sang-Woo Rhee, *Unification for Co-prosperity: A Pragmatic Formula for Inter-Korean Political Integration* (Seoul: Nanam, 1993) (in Korean); and some popular novels now abundant in Korea.

[26] Yang, et al., *The Road to Reunification*, pp. 153ff.

[27] It is likely that such moves may be accompanied by increasing contacts with the South, particularly the reunion of separated families.

[28] C.f., see Rhee, *Unification for Co-prosperity*, pp. 191–192.

[29] Assuming that North Korea successfully reforms its economic system and grows 10% annually, and that the South Korean economy becomes saturated at a 5% per year growth, it would take nearly 40 years for North Korean incomes to reach half of South Korean incomes. Still, with the population twice as big as the North's, South Korea's GNP would be about four times bigger than that of North Korea.

[30] Table 3 is reconstructed from Tables 10 through 12, from Ku, et al., *Korean Reunification Scenarios*, pp. 45–47.

[31] Cf., see Thomas J. Christensen and Jack Snyder, "Chain Gangs and Passed Bucks: Predicting Alliance Patterns in Multipolarity," *International Organization*, Vol. 44, No. 2 (Spring 1990).

[32] Robert Cox, "Multilateralism and World Order," *Review of International Studies*, Vol. 18 (1992).

[33] John Ruggie, "Multilateralism: The Anatomy of an Institution," in Ruggie, ed., *Multilateralism Matters*, p. 11.

[34] Ibid. The term "diffuse reciprocity" is first used in Robert O. Keohane, "Reciprocity in International Relations," *International Organization*, Vol. 40, No 1 (Winter 1985). See also Taehyun Kim and Chae-Han Kim, "Diffuse Reciprocity and Theories of International Cooperation: A Note on a Research Program," paper presented at the annual conference of International Studies Association, Chicago, February 1995, for related arguments.

[35] Robert Axelrod and Robert Keohane, "Achieving Cooperation Under Anarchy: Strategies and Institutions," in David A. Baldwin, ed., *Neorealism and Neoliberalism: The Contemporary Debate* (New York: Columbia University Press, 1993), pp. 91–94. If actors pass up short-term interests for longer-term returns, it is another expression of "refuse reciprocity," which multilateralism offers. See Kim and Kim, "Diffuse Reciprocity and Theories of International Cooperation"; and Ruggie, "Multilateralism," p. 22.

[36] Ruggie, "Multilateralism," p. 11.

[37] See Taehyun Kim, "South Korean Perspectives on North Korean Nuclear Question," *Mershon International Studies Review*, Vol. 40, Supplement 2 (October 1996) for further discussion of this point. In a recent survey conducted by the Sejong Institute in October 1997, Korean people were asked to rate North Korea on a seven-point scale ranging from 1 for "pure enemy" and 7 for "pure brother." The distribution of responses is bell-shaped, with the mean of 4.48 and mode of 5—3.4%, 7.1%, 11.6%, 25.1%, 29.3%, 15.9%, and 7.6% from 1 to 7, respectively. I assume that the mean would be lower if the survey had been conducted after the arrest of the spy couple in November. See Taehyun Kim, "Perceptions and Policy Attitude of South Korean Public Toward the North," *Sejong Nonchong* [Collection of Papers] (Seoul: The Sejong Institute, 1998; in Korean).

[38] Taehyun Kim, "Rethinking Security in the Korean Peninsula: Inter-Korean Relations as a System of Simultaneous Equations of Security, Peace and Unification," in Jaemahn Suh, ed., *Korea and Middle East in Changing World Order* (Seoul: Institute of Middle East Studies, Hankuk University of Foreign Studies, 1996), p. 264.

[39] An attractive alternative might be such a subgroup meeting within the context of APEC. The APEC is at the summit level, allowing more comprehensive cooperation. Also, such a meeting in the APEC context will allow issue-linkage, another expression of diffuse reciprocity and a catalyst for international cooperation. Yet, because APEC is riddled with many of its own (economic) problems and two of the proposed members, i.e., Russia and North Korea, are not APEC members, the practical value of this option is generally doomed. See Yong-Chool Ha and Taehyun Kim, "Reflections on APEC: A Korean

Perspective," in Donald Hellmann and Kenneth Pyle, eds., *From APEC to Xanadu: Creating a Viable Community in the Post-Cold War Pacific* (New York: M. E. Sharpe, 1997) for a discussion of the security ramifications of APEC. See Ernst Haas, "Why Collaborate: Issue-Linkage and International Regimes," *World Politics*, Vol. 32, No. 3 (April 1980) for a discussion of issue-linkage as facilitator of international cooperation, and Kim and Kim, "Diffuse Reciprocity and Theories of International Cooperation," for the discussion of issue-linkage as an expression of diffuse reciprocity.

[40] It has been convincingly demonstrated that multilateral cooperation tends to generate "defensive cooperation" by even relative gains maximizers. See Duncan Snidal, "Relative Gains and the Pattern of Cooperation," *American Political Science Review*, Vol. 85, No. 3 (September 1991); and Duncan Snidal, "International Cooperation Among Relative Gains Maximizers," *International Studies Quarterly*, Vol. 35, No. 4 (December 1991).

Prospects for Japan–Korea Defense Cooperation:

Partners or Rivals

By Otsuka Umio,
Commander, Japan Maritime Self-Defense Forces*

Overview[1]

Since the end of the Cold War, relations between the military of Japan and the Republic of Korea (ROK) have shown dramatic improvement. Not only have the two defense ministries held dialogues on a regular basis, but also their navies have exchanged port visits. Following World War II and throughout the Cold War, Japan and ROK were both key members of the Western alliance in the East Asia region, but they have never been military partners. The growing cooperation between the two military establishments stems mainly from an imminent threat to both countries: North Korea.

Historically, with regard to security, Korea has watched Japan with suspicion, whereas Japan's basic attitude toward Korea has been one of indifference.[2] Improved relations between the two countries are the

**The views expressed are those of the author and do not necessarily represent the views of the Japanese Maritime Self-Defense Force or any other Japanese government organization.*

result of the security dynamics in the region, of a will to create better relations. But although the current Japanese–ROK relationship is largely based on the perception of North Korea as a threat, it also results from insecurity about what will happen when the North Korean threat has dissipated—a scenario that seems increasingly likely.

There is much debate about the future of the Korean Peninsula[3] centering on whether reunification will occur in the near future or the division will endure, what the process of reunification will be, and what the nature of a reunified country will be if that becomes a reality. While the future of the Korean Peninsula is very uncertain, it is now apparent that the South will dominate the style and pace of reunification when it happens. This means that if reunification occurs, future military relations between Japan and Korea (the ROK until reunification and the Unified Korea in the post-reunification period) will fundamentally be an extension of the current relations between Japan and the ROK.

This paper assesses the prospects of defense cooperation between Japan and Korea by (1) drawing on strategic relations between Japan and Korea in historical context; (2) reviewing the defense efforts of both countries, including their bilateral defense cooperation; (3) identifying their common security interests and establishing the need for defense cooperation; and finally, (4) suggesting policy recommendations for the future.

Japan–Korea Relations: External Factors

Although Korea suffered from Japanese piracy before the fifth century, the first encounter between their national military forces took place in the seventh century, when Japan undertook an expedition to the Korean Peninsula in support of Kudara (Baik Jei in Korean), one of the three countries that sought to unite the peninsula by conquering others. Korea attacked Japan only once in the thirteenth century, but this was as a proxy for China, which was then under Mongol rule (Yuan Dynasty). In the sixteenth century, Japan sent an expeditionary force to Korea, which was defeated. Korea, however, exhausted as a result of this war with Japan, capitulated to Chinese rule. In the late nineteenth and early twentieth centuries, Korea served as a battleground for power struggles between Japan, China, and Russia.[4] In this century, Japan annexed Korea in 1910 and did not surrender control until Japan lost the war in 1945.

Summarizing this history, Japan has always been a direct threat to Korea, whereas Korea as a nation has never been perceived as a threat to Japan. However, the geostrategic proximity of the Korean Peninsula has historically been problematic for Japan. The constant threat to Japan's security has not been Korea itself, but rather the powers seeking control over the peninsula that were hostile to Japan.[5] Today, given the unchanged geostrategic situation that on the one hand, Japan's island chain blocks the exit to the open sea for Korea, and on the other, that the Korean Peninsula represents a "dagger at the heart" of Japan, naturally the two nations are concerned with each other's political and military action.

During the Cold War, however, Japan and the ROK, both as members of a Western alliance, confronted the Soviet-backed Eastern threat on the front line of the Far East. The two bilateral alliances of U.S.–Japan and U.S.–ROK indirectly linked Japan and the ROK as if they were partners through the United States, even though no formal military relations existed. In reality, numerous political, economic, and cultural confrontations occurred between the two.

International relations have affected the relations between Japan and the ROK since the end of World War II. After the overtly hostile policy of Syngman Rhee toward Japan, President Park Chung Hee pushed ahead with diplomatic normalization with Japan in the face of South Korea's need for Japanese capital. This capital was required for the economic development of South Korea in the face of the North's economic superiority.[6] Tokyo's pursuit of an autonomous security policy, derived from skepticism toward U.S.–Asian policy, the result of the Nixon Doctrine, and U.S.–Sino diplomatic negotiations without any consultation with Japan, promoted its relationship with North Korea. In the mid 1970s, the communist victory in Vietnam and North Korea's belligerence toward capitalist states altered the relationship between Tokyo and Seoul to one of collaboration. As the intensity of the Cold War heightened in the 1980s, Japan-Korea policy collaboration enjoyed its heyday. However, while Seoul's Nordpolitik continued after the end of the Cold War, Japan attempted to normalize diplomatic relations with the North, which refueled the South's suspicion about Japanese intentions. Growing pressure to improve relations was a reaction to the North Korean unclear weapons crisis, and since then Japan and the ROK have enjoyed a firmly grounded cooperative relationship.

There have also been domestic political issues that have in most cases negatively affected the bilateral relationship. Rising nationalism in both Japan and the ROK, stirring up the deeply imbedded legacy of distrust among both peoples, has made the bilateral relationship complicated. Historical issues have been resolved at least at the government level; however, much suspicion still remains among the Korean public, and consequently, counter-distrust exists among the Japanese. Further, some problems that the two governments have not yet resolved, such as disputed territorial issues involving islands, continue to fan nationalist sentiments. Sentiments based on cultural distrust are easily manipulated and used domestically by certain political factions in both countries. Unless the people of Japan and the ROK successfully overcome their distrust of each other, emotional factors will continue to play a significant destabilizing role in the bilateral relationship. Although there have been some positive examples for future relations,[7] much concern remains about the residue of the historical antipathy between the two countries.

The status of bilateral relations between Japan and the ROK since the end of World War II, whether good or bad, has resulted from the relations of each with other countries, especially North Korea, rather than from relations between themselves. The international situation has been the key determinant of the Japanese-Korean relationship.

Even with the Cold War ended—with the collapse of the bipolar systems of the East-West confrontation and the disappearance of the threat of global war—a divided Korea still poses the threat of a regional war that will significantly affect the ROK and Japanese security. Therefore, the stability of the Korean Peninsula has emerged as the key factor in regional stability. This became most apparent when the North Korean regime created the nuclear weapons and ballistic missiles crisis in the early 1990s. In response to the uncertainty in the region, Japan and the ROK embarked on policies emphasizing the development of military cooperation.

So long as the North Korean threat exists, there is an exceptional opportunity to develop cooperative security relations. However, once that threat dissipates, a new security environment will emerge that will be dependent on the conditions under which the North Korean threat has been eliminated. The drastic change in the regional security condition concomitant with the disappearance of the North's threat will affect the relationship between Tokyo and Seoul. To build a hedge against this uncertainty, Japan and the ROK must develop closer consultation that looks well beyond the extinction of the North's threat to the issues that will emerge following reunification. Not only is this necessary, but conditions are favorable for mutual discussion. The ROK is still immersed militarily in dealing with the North's threat, but it has also begun speculating about future strategy in the context of regional security for the post-reunification period.

Defense Relations Between Japan and the ROK

Japan's Defense Policy

Japan's Self-Defense Forces (JSDF) were established under American occupation after World War II to fill the vacuum created by the shift of U.S. forces to the Korean War and were originally designated to perform constabulary missions. Because of public antipathy to the military after the experiences before and during World War II, as well as because of the new power of civilians inherent in the Japanese Constitution, the JSDF has been completely isolated from domestic politics as well as from the foreign-policy making process. With Japan as an ally of the United States, the JSDF has cooperated closely with U.S. forces in the Pacific since its inception. In this context, the JSDF came to play a crucial role in the Western alliance in the Far East against the Soviet Union throughout the Cold War. Because of constraints imposed by the Japanese Constitution, this role has been exclusively defensive without any projected capability such as aircraft carriers, bombers, or long-range missiles. Japan's geostrategic position, which blocked the Soviet navy's access to the Pacific Ocean, made Japan a great contributor to the West's abilities to deter the Soviet menace.

Global Security

The Gulf War in 1990–1991 created much domestic controversy in Japan. The political debate raged over whether Japan should take up the burden for world peace by sending the JSDF overseas in support of the United Nations Peace-Keeping Operations (UNPKO). Although Japan contributed $13 billion, it was not appreciated; rather, it was criticized as "checkbook diplomacy." In the aftermath of the Gulf War, after a great deal of debate, the Diet finally passed the International Peace Cooperation Law in 1992, and the first peacekeeping forces were dispatched to Cambodia the same year.[8] The JSDF has since played a role in global activities as an instrument of Japanese foreign policy.

Regional Security

The trend toward an expanded role for the JSDF was enhanced in 1995 when the new National Defense Program Outline (NDPO) was submitted. The previous NDPO was formulated in 1976 to clarify the future modularity of Japan's defense capability, based upon the premises of Cold War situations. The new NDPO of 1995 was submitted in response to the changing security environment in the post–Cold War era. It prescribed, along with national defense, responses to large-scale disasters and various other situations, as well as contributions to creation of a more stable security environment, as future roles of the JSDF.[9] The JSDF was assigned missions to (1) cope with situations that could seriously affect Japan's peace and security; (2) actively implement international peace-cooperation activities; and (3) pursue promotion of security dialogues and exchanges, and cooperation in arms control and disarmament efforts.

With the North Korean nuclear and missile crises in the early 1990s as one trigger, Japan and the United States began negotiations to reaffirm the U.S.–Japan Security Arrangement to adapt it to the situations of the post–Cold War era. As a result, a joint declaration was submitted at the summit meeting in April 1996, which reaffirmed that Japan would maintain the alliance with the United States as the basis of Japan's defense in the post–Cold War era. Next, the Guidelines for U.S.–Japan Defense Cooperation were renewed in September 1997. The old guidelines focused mainly on combined actions in response to an armed attack against Japan, with only few provisions described for cooperation in the regional crisis. The new guidelines added more detailed areas for cooperation under normal circumstances such as peacekeeping operations, humanitarian assistance, and security dialogues, and clearly describe in which areas each country will cooperate in situations close to Japan that will affect Japan's peace and security.[10] Although pending domestic legislation is required to legitimize actions conducted by the JSDF and make the guidelines effective, Japan now has a clear vision of its role in regional security and the role of the JSDF.

South Korea's Concern

There exists some fear in Koreans that Japan is preparing to establish the capability to project power in Asia.[11] Until 1992, the Republic of Korea *Defense White Paper* had assessed the Japanese defense posture with negative connotations such as that "[Japan] is gradually trying to change its territorial defense concept to a more aggressive forward defense by interpreting more broadly the concepts of command and control and territorial defense."[12] Although the Japanese believe that their constitution strictly restrains military growth, some Koreans were made uneasy when the Japanese Maritime Self-Defense Force (JMSDF) dispatched minesweeping forces to the Persian Gulf to secure the international sealanes after the Gulf War.[13] It appears that Korean distrust, if not actual suspicion, of Japan's motives for international involvement still remains.

The U.S. Role for Japan

Japan, though defeated in World War II and occupied after the war by the United States, appreciates U.S. initiatives in the course of restoration from the war and reentry to the international community. A majority of

Japanese believe that the U.S.–Japan security arrangement has supported today's economic prosperity in Japan.[14] The Japanese government sees the alliance as functioning effectively and supports enhancing the credibility of the alliance.[15] Keeping the U.S. presence in the region is of vital interest to Japan, and Japan, therefore, has provided bases and implemented Host Nation Support for the continued presence of U.S. forces. Although most Japanese officials, especially in the security community, think that the U.S.–Japan alliance is a given condition for the defense of Japan, there is also a movement to oppose U.S. military presence in Japan. This is especially true in Okinawa, the smallest among 51 prefectures, where some 75 percent of all U.S. bases in Japan are located. The government of Japan, in cooperation with the U.S. government, established in 1995 the Special Action Committee on Facilities and Areas in Okinawa (SACO) and is exerting maximum effort to resolve the problems in Okinawa to sustain the U.S. presence.

China and Japanese Security

Japan's policy toward China has been somewhat different from that of other Western countries. Japan has tried to engage and accommodate China; even after the Tiananmen massacres, the government of Japan has tried to prevent Chinese isolation.[16] China, because of its geopolitical position, has directly affected the security of Japan throughout history. However, in the 1990s Japan has increasingly developed a perception of China as a threat, based on China's maritime expansion in the south and East China Seas and its claim over the Senkaku Islands, to its increasing its defense budget in secrecy, and to its nuclear experiments in spite of protests from other countries. China's missile exercises in March 1996, intimidating voters in Taiwan's presidential election, underscored the Chinese-threat argument in Japan. Some data now show that the Japanese people consider that China, after North Korea, is second-most-likely to pose a military threat to Japan.[17]

North Korea and Japanese Security

Although Japan was implicitly involved in the confrontation along the 38th parallel in the Korean Peninsula—playing the role of a logistic base for the UN Forces in accordance with the Status Agreement of UN Forces of 1954—the present perception of North Korea as a threat was ignited by suspicions of the North's development of nuclear weapons and ballistic missiles in the early 1990s. These potential capabilities pose a direct threat to the security of Japan. In addition, closer attention is now being paid to the direct and indirect effects of a collapse, by either explosion or implosion, of the North's regime. These include potential risk to the lives and assets of Japanese in South Korea, the turmoil that would be caused by a massive flow of refugees, the possibility of mines affecting the sea-lanes, and the estimated logistic support for U.S. forces committed to the situation on the peninsula. Though not aimed at specific scenarios, the new defense guidelines take the potential crisis in the Korean Peninsula into consideration.

The ROK's Defense Policy

The legacy of the ROK Forces (ROKF) goes back to the Korean War, after which the ROK introduced a large-scale standing army based on conscription against Korea's traditional aspect for its nonmilitary heritage.[18] Following the key role the military played when Syngman Rhee became the first president, the ROKF was deeply involved in the domestic politics of the ROK until the demilitarization of politics by President Roh Tae Woo, starting in 1988.[19]

Since the creation of the demilitarized zone along the 38th parallel in 1953, the ROKF has been prepared primarily for the threat from the North, and North Korea remains the main enemy of the ROK.[20] Maintaining sufficient deterrence against the North's aggression, together with U.S. forces in Korea, has been the main task of the ROKF. As a consequence, the current level of the ROKF is maintained to counter an all-out attack by the North.[21]

Global Security

Since the simultaneous entry of both South and North Korea into the UN, a new dimension has been added to the mission of the ROKF: UNPKO. The first South Korean mission under UNPKO was to send an engineering unit to Somalia in 1993, and the ROK has since participated in operations in the western Sahara, Georgia, and Kashmir. Participant in UNPKO indirectly led to strengthening the deterrence on the northern border because the armistice is maintained under UN auspices,[22] and it also helped the ROK develop an active role in maintaining peace and stability[23] deterrence on the Korean Peninsula as well as engagement in efforts for world peace and stability.

Regional Security

A new aspect of the security debate in the ROK has emerged: the idea that the ROK should prepare for future situations, including the post-reunification era, in which the armed forces may be employed against a wide range of external threats.[24] Given Korea's geostrategic location where the interests of four major powers in the region, the United States, Japan, China, and Russia, intersect, and the growing South Korea status as a regional power based on its economy, the ROK has begun seeking its own regional role. The ROK government holds the view that the ROKF needs to create a future-oriented defense policy and a relevant posture that can cope with uncertainties in the strategic environment.[25] There are many opinions on how to deal with security issues in the post-reunification era, ranging from maintaining the current bilateral alliance with the United States to expanding military capability for unilateral defense. What is certain is that in addition to deterrence of North Korea, assuming a role in regional security has become an issue for the ROKF.

Japan's Concern

As a result of its regional defense strategy, the ROKF has introduced weapon systems consistent with an expanded role. To promote self-reliant defense, the ROK government has pursued indigenous arms production for "Korean Defense in Korean Hands."[26] The ROK acquired submarines from Germany in 1987 and P-3C maritime patrol aircraft from the United States in 1990. It has started indigenous production of submarines and KDX destroyers, and has licensed production of F-16 fighters. Some American observers believe that Seoul should focus on the North's threat by procuring weapons systems for counter-artillery or coastal defense instead of spending on power-projection weapons not directly related to the North's threat. Some Japanese defense officials believe that Seoul is acquiring weapons systems capable of countering the JSDF in order to seek hegemony when the U.S. forces leave the region.[27] It appears that distrust of Korea has begun to emerge among Japanese regarding Korea's intentions for future national defense.

The United States and the ROK

According to Don Oberdorfer, Koreans, liberated by the United States from Japanese annexation at the end of World War II, feel they have been betrayed twice by the United States: first, when then U.S. Secretary of

State William Taft approved Japan's domination of Korea in a secret agreement in 1905; and second, when Americans drew the line along the 38th parallel in 1945.[28] However, Koreans now trust the United States as honest broker in Asia because the United States is the only major power that has not militarily invaded Korea. In the regional context beyond the North's threat, while Japanese view the U.S. presence as stabilizer of the region, Koreans see the United States as balancer and moderator. Therefore, the regional major powers, Japan and China, most likely, would engage in an accelerated arms race were the United States to withdraw from the region.[29] Among the defense elite in the ROK, the consensus has been that the U.S. presence should be maintained after the North's threat has disappeared. However, the military structure should be adjusted to reflect the changed situation. But there is also strong opinion in South Korea that it will not be able to depend on the U.S. security umbrella, and that therefore, the ROK should build up stronger forces. In the navy's case, for example, this would include acquiring aircraft carriers and Aegis destroyers to enable the ROK to act as a balancing power between regional powers, especially between Japan and China.[30] In contrast to Japan where the JSDF is trying to strengthen its coordination with U.S. forces through joint operations, the ROKF is seeking a more independent approach through the "Koreanization of Korean defense."[31] The diversified sources of weapons procurement reinforce this observation. Considering that the ROK is a sovereign state that has become a world-class middle power through its growing economy, this independence is an understandable movement. However, from the U.S. and Japanese viewpoints, questions are emerging about where the ROK and a unified Korea in the future are heading.

China and the ROK

China, fearing U.S. hegemony in the region, has officially criticized the U.S.–ROK alliance. China, however, has been accepting the alliance tacitly because it protects the stability of the Korean Peninsula and constrains Japan.[32] Nevertheless, if after reunification Korea still maintains the alliance with the presence of U.S. forces in the Korean Peninsula, China is bound to feel uncomfortable.[33] For the Chinese, a strong U.S.–ROK alliance is acceptable only under the current northeast Asian security framework. Further, while the majority of the ROK defense elite have started seeking closer military cooperation with Japan, they are, at the same time, afraid of provoking China by enhancing relations with Japan.[34] Aware of this, the ROK is more than sensitive to China's perception of events. It believes that China likes the status quo, and that unless provoked by outside players, China will be a supportive power for the reunification of Korea.[35] Compared with that of Japan, the ROK *Defense White Paper* makes little mention of Chinese naval activities in the South China Sea where Korean sea lines of communications (SLOC) pass, or about the Chinese missile exercises around the Taiwan Strait. The ROK paper states that there is nothing to be concerned about in the Chinese military buildup. Because of these differing reactions to China, the issue of relations with China should be the most carefully managed aspect in developing defense cooperation between Japan and the ROK.

North Korea and the ROK

Although the citizens of both North and South Korea are the same Koreans, and the reunification of the country is their earnest wish, North Korea has been the main enemy of the ROK since the Korean War, and the fierce antagonism between the two Koreas remains undiminished.[36] Over the past forty-five years, the generations have changed in both Koreas, and the majority of Koreans do not remember Korea before the division. Having seen the aftermath of German unification, some South Koreans even do not want the reunification, which may impose a tremendous burden in the South.[37] South Koreans do not necessarily have a consensus about Korea's overall future, other than that the clear and present danger posed by the North must end.

Japan–ROK Defense Relations

Japan and the ROK have been indirectly connected through their bilateral alliances with the United States, although they themselves have no bilateral security arrangement. The JMSDF and the ROK Navy (ROKN) both participated in RIMPAC after the ROKN's entry in 1990, a multinational naval exercise initiated by the United States. Because the JMSDF has not been allowed to conduct exercises with navies of countries other than the United States, due to a constraint on the interpretation of Japan's constitution against exercising collective defense rights, this has been the only opportunity for both countries to have military-to-military operational contact, during the Cold War. Although various bilateral contacts started in the 1990s between Japan and the ROK, RIMPAC is still the only exercise in which both military forces operate on the same stage with Japan, the ROK, and the United States committed to the trilateral maneuver.

During the Cold War, while the United States and the ROK were attempting to engage Japan in U.S.–ROK bilateral relations, Japan was completely negative. Although Japanese Prime Minister Sato stated in the joint communiqué of 1969 with U.S. President Nixon that the security of the Korean Peninsula is essential to Japan, the Japanese official stance was to back down. There has been no military commitment since then except for some basic information and personnel exchanges held routinely since diplomatic relations were restored in 1965. The reason is the Japanese fear of becoming entrapped in a regional alliance system[38] as well as hesitation based on their historical legacy.

In the 1990s, beginning with the initial visit of the ROK Chairman, Joint Staff Council, and the visit of Japan's Director General of Defense (the first such visit since 1979), exchanges between defense officials have increased dramatically. The exchange of Defense Institute students started in 1990. Since 1994, the heads of Japanese and South Korean Defense Ministries have made reciprocal visits on a regular basis and annual meetings have been held for working-level defense officials. There have been tangible outcomes such as an agreement on the prevention of accidental mid-air collision of aircraft from the air forces of both countries, and reciprocal port visits of their respective naval training squadrons. As a result, "the current defense relationship between Japan and the ROK is the most successful among other relationships between these two nations."[39]

There are several reasons for the recent increase in defense cooperation between Japan and South Korea. First, the possibility of the North's explosion or implosion has become stronger, and both countries need to cope with this regional issue. Second, the declining power of the North and the South's rising power have made reunification a real possibility. The ROK has started thinking about a post-reunification security environment in which Japan as well as united Korea will play significant roles in the regional security. Third, the ROK, in particular, has been concerned with the withdrawal of the U.S. presence from the region. After the reunification, it is likely that the United States will reduce, if not withdraw, its presence in northeast Asia. Fourth, China, with its increased military capability and operational area, has created concerns for both Japan and the ROK as well as the United States. On that basis, then, will Japan and the ROK forge a cooperative defense relationship from now on? Preparing to cope with the potential crisis caused by North Korea is the immediate priority, and that effort has already started. But the real necessity for long-term ROK–Japanese cooperation lies in the uncertainty about what will happen after the North's threat is gone.

Common Security Interests and the Goal of Defense Cooperation

Today's economic prosperity in Japan and the ROK was brought about by the regional stability that was sustained even during the Cold War. The defense policy of both countries to commit to regional security demonstrates their will to maintain this stability. Hence, for both countries, maintaining regional stability is clearly the common interest. Japan's role or function as a logistical base in case of crisis is critical to operational support to the United States and the ROK. Japan will be even more important in the post-crisis phase, not only with its economic support but also in operationally supporting a U.S. presence as a stabilizer in the region. The Koreans should determine the Korean issue. Therefore, Japan needs to consult with the ROK to keep abreast of plans for the ultimate reunification. What if Japan and the ROK are not cooperative and the distrust among both people remains entrenched vis-à-vis the potential crisis in the Korean Peninsula and its aftermath? The answer will be increased uncertainty about regional security.

The following security-related goals[40] are critical for both Japan and the ROK to achieve and sustain their common interest: regional stability.

- Prevent North Korea from exploding or imploding (no "hard landing").
- Maintain U.S. presence in the region.
- Ensure freedom of navigation.
- Engage China so that it becomes a responsible regional player.
- Support peaceful resolution of the Taiwan Strait issue.
- Support multilateral security dialogues and efforts in the region.
- Prevent the proliferation of weapons of mass destruction (WMD).
- Support the development of the Russian Far East, nurturing its democratic development and its emergence as a constructive regional player.

Some of these issues have a different character from the perspectives of Japan and Korea, owing largely to differences in their national interests and their capability to pursue certain policies.

North Korea

Japan has its own trouble with the North: Japanese kidnapped by North Korean agents. Japan's diplomatic effort to resolve the kidnapping issue with the North could be seen by the ROK government as an effort to keep Korea divided. South Koreans want to keep the Japanese voice over the Korean issue minimal, if not mute.

U.S. Presence

The primary role of the U.S. forces in Korea is to deter the North's aggression, whereas in Japan the U.S. role is to maintain regional stability. This difference in the current role of U.S. presence in the two countries makes it difficult to share a common picture of future U.S. presence.

Freedom of Navigation

The prosperity of Japan and the ROK is sustained by free trade, so for both countries, freedom of navigation is crucial. The JMSDF is already maintaining sea-lane defense capability up to 1,000 nautical miles from Japan, whereas the ROKN has only coastal defense capability. Thus, the ROK's effort to forge a naval power capable of securing freedom of navigation will be a political as well as an economic burden.

China

Both Japan and ROK are surely aware that their cooperation should not invoke China's suspicion of being contained. However, while Japan cannot overlook the fact that China would have overwhelming influence on the Korean Peninsula, the ROK, with its historical sympathy to China, appreciates and even considers indispensable China's influence over the North for the peaceful solution of the Korean issue.

Taiwan

The Taiwan Strait Crisis in 1996 invoked Japanese skepticism about China. On the other hand, the Chinese feared that Japan would support containment of China because Japan was the home port of U.S. Navy aircraft carriers dispatched during the crisis. China has consistently criticized the new Guidelines for U.S.–Japan Defense Cooperation with regard to its geographical interpretation of whether Taiwan is included or not, although both the United States and Japan have repeatedly explained that the Guidelines are based on a functional rather than geographical concept. Given its sensitivity to relations with China, the ROK relatively recently switched its diplomatic relations from Taipei to Beijing, and it will maximize its efforts not to antagonize China, even if another crisis occurs around Taiwan where the ROK's SLOC pass.

Regional Multilateralism

Both Japan and the ROK depend for their security on an alliance with United States. Based on this bilateral defense system, Japan seeks regional multilateral cooperation to enhance regional stability, whereas the ROK needs it for a peaceful solution to the Korean problem because reunification will not become reality without the consensus of all regional powers.

Nuclear Issues

Neither Japan nor the ROK have nuclear weapons. Also, both countries have formalized their reunification by the Three Nuclear Principles in the case of Japan (that Japan will neither possess, introduce, nor produce nuclear weapons), and by signing, along with North Korea, The Declaration on Denuclearization of the Korean Peninsula. Japan, by conducting research to decide whether to adopt the Theater Missile Defense system with its advanced technology, is already committed to cooperating on the regional nuclear issue with the United States, whereas the ROK is not because of limited capability.

Several basic obstacles impede defense cooperation between Japan and the ROK:

- embedded distrust and rising nationalism among their respective peoples.
- Japan's lack of consensus for defense cooperation, derived from the constitutional constraint.
- potential pitfall to establishing a lasting U.S.–ROK alliance for secure deterrence against the North as a result of discussing a future U.S. presence.

How should Japan and the ROK cooperate militarily to support their common interests by minimizing the difference in interests and hedging against future contingencies? First, and most urgent, is to implement confidence building measures (CBM) to overcome the fundamental obstacle between Japan and the ROK: distrust. As a part of this effort, both countries should pursue cooperative measures to contribute to the regional stability by spelling out and addressing the objectives just outlined.

Policy Recommendations

Given the existing framework for bilateral defense cooperation, such as exchanges of high-level defense personnel, regular consultations among defense officials, exchanges of students and defense studies, and exchanges between units—resulting from years of effort after decades of noncontacts—"vehicles" for pursuing cooperation have been almost settled. Along with efforts to strengthen the existing framework, how to promote future cooperation is the main agenda: what should be the means and how should they be implemented, based on the current opportunity for U.S.–Japan–ROK trilateral dialogue? In addition, a multilateral framework with more nations should also be considered, but it will first be necessary to reinforce the current framework by reassuring the regional players. The bottom line of defense cooperation between Japan and the ROK is to eliminate distrust, develop confidence, and sustain regional stability, including coordination for responding to crises. The North Korean issue, the most immediate concern, should be addressed not only bilaterally but also trilaterally by including the United States, and then multilaterally by including China and Russia. This issue, however, is related to the long-term question of how to achieve the peaceful coexistence of North and South Korea without damaging regional stability.

The following activities address both short- and long-term requirements of defense cooperation between Japan and the ROK.

Dialogue for Policy Consultation

First and foremost, the governments of Japan and the ROK, as well as the JSDF and the ROKF, should start with consultation to formulate policy for arriving at the common goal of defense cooperation. The military-to-military contact between Japan and the ROK is not incidental to their involvement with the United States. Both sides should proceed one step further to substantial cooperation from mere "contact." A series of cooperative efforts should follow carefully designed to achieve the common goal: building mutual confidence and seeking long-term regional stability based on this confidence. Once overall policy is settled at the national level, it should be followed by regular exchanges between the military leaders of the two countries. For example, chiefs and officers in charge of policy planning for each branch of the armed forces could meet with their counterparts, as could the commanders of equivalent military units. Such exchanges will help consolidate mutual policy for defense cooperation.

Confidence-Building Measures

The bottom-line goal of defense cooperation is to eliminate distrust and build confidence. Confidence built through such fundamental cooperation will help prevent other national problems from escalating to damage the bilateral relationship. This has been demonstrated by the examples of U.S.–Japan and U.S.–ROK military alliances. The following activities[41] by the two countries will promote transparency and contribute to confidence building by:

- encouraging mutual visits by naval vessels and military aircraft.
- promoting exchanges among various ranking officers and among military institutions.
- notifying each other of major military activities.
- inviting and accepting observers for military exercises.
- exchanging information concerning the procurement and retirement of military assets.

Response to the Crisis in the Korean Peninsula

As previously mentioned in the new Guidelines, the United States and Japan recently agreed on various points of defense cooperation in the event of a crisis that affects the peace and security of Japan. Although the Guidelines are not aimed at a specific area, this agreement must be implemented if a crisis occurs in the Korean Peninsula. The JSDF operations are mainly the rear-area support for the U.S. forces. However, in a crisis in Korea, where thousands of Japanese civilians are living, Japan could be forced to make a commitment if the ROK accepts it. If this happens, operational coordination between the JSDF and the ROKF will be critical. There are still many domestic political problems with this kind of cooperation in Japan fundamentally derived from constitutional constraints. However, Japan should advance now to the next step of coordination with the ROK, preferably in a trilateral setting with the United States playing a leading role. Moreover, as a hedge against Chinese suspicion, a consultative mechanism that includes the United States, Japan, the ROK, and China should be suggested. The following are issues to be addressed in the trilateral dialogue initiated by the United States regarding the division of responsibility:

- assignment of ports and airports to use for Noncombatant Evacuation Operation (NEO).
- protection of evacuees at the ports or airports in case of NEO: who and how.
- protection of vessels for NEO in and out of Korean territorial waters

including mine countermeasures (the ROK armed forces is likely to be completely occupied in national defense rather than in protecting evacuees, considering the current structure of the ROK Navy and Air Force.): who and where; (NEO is particularly important since Japan would be directly concerned in the discussions because of its citizens in Korea).

- procedures for intelligence exchange: what, when, and how.
- Search and Rescue (SAR): who, where, and how.
- Maritime Interdiction Operation (MIO): who and where.

Humanitarian Assistance

In case of major natural disasters, military forces have effective assets to provide medical support, transport food, goods, personnel, and water supplies. Military organizations are also useful in coping with environmental disasters, such as oil spills from a shipwreck in international waters. For example, the JSDF has been maintaining preparedness to respond to major disasters overseas in accordance with the Disaster Relief Law of 1992.[42] Japan and the ROK, being neighboring countries, can effectively cooperate in this area. Both governments can start with politically less-controversial items, such as SAR or medical support activities. When the situation allows, transport of personnel by JSDF assets dispatched to the ROK should be considered as the next step. The possibility exists for multilaterally coordinated operations in case of major disasters in the region. An example would be disasters along the coast of the Russian Far East, including the Sakhalin and Kuril Islands where both Japan and the ROK have economic interests and where the Russians seem to lack the necessary assets for the relief operations. In cases like this, multilateral humanitarian assistance can be an option. Considering the current domestic political blocks to bilateral defense in both Japan and the ROK, humanitarian operations are the easiest approach to developing defense cooperation with the least domestic resistance.

U.S. Presence in the Region

The North Korean problem, with its declaration of withdrawal from NPT and its alleged production of nuclear weapons and development of ballistic missiles, has grown from the peninsula issue to a broader regional one. The ongoing U.S.–Japan–ROK defense cooperation originated in response to this issue. After years of informal contacts, formal trilateral meetings by defense officials started in 1997. Although the crisis in the

Korean Peninsula has been the main issue for the trilateral meetings,[43] the meetings have promoted mutual understanding between Japan and the ROK. Considering the fact that "throughout the Cold War, the U.S.–Japan alliance has functioned as a base for regional security policy, while the U.S.–ROK alliance has primarily functioned as a deterrent against North Korea,"[44] the manner of commitment of the United States, which both Japan and the ROK foresee as continuing after the North's threat has disappeared, would change.

The United States, Japan, and the ROK should start consulting on this issue well before the regional situation moves to the next stage: demise of the North's threat. Once the threat has gone, U.S. domestic pressure and Korean nationalism could force a reduction of the U.S. presence. In Japan, budgetary difficulty in funding host nation support could cause sympathy for the reduction of U.S. presence. If the present structure of the U.S. forces in East Asia were adjusted, the core of the future forces would be naval units and some air forces stationed in Japan. As long as the unified Korea maintains a security relationship with the United States, the need for consultation among the United States, Japan, and the ROK will continue. Now that the ROK has begun to think about its future relations with the United States, it is important to start discussions regarding the posture of the U.S. presence in the future. The U.S. presence is a key issue for both Japan and the ROK in both short-term and long-term agendas. The two countries should consult and coordinate in this regard. The U.S.–Japan–ROK trilateral mechanism offers a way to address this issue. It should be used, therefore, not only to cope with the short-term concern posed by the North's military threat, but also to consult about the future of a U.S. presence in the region in order to deal with the uncertainty.

Freedom of Navigation

For Japan and the ROK, both heavily dependent on marine transport for raw materials and the flow of commodities, freedom of navigation is crucial for their economic prosperity and even for survival. Japan has announced since the 1980s that it has a naval capability to protect sea-lanes within 1,000 nautical miles from home. Under its Exclusively Defense-Oriented Policy,[45] Japan no longer possesses power-projection equipment such as aircraft carriers and long-range bombers. The ROK has naval capability only for protecting coastal waters. However, its recent efforts to strengthen its navy are significant. The ROKN has been constructing a submarine fleet, introducing modern maritime-patrol aircraft, and indigenously producing destroyers. Looking beyond the reunification, the ROKN has begun building the capability to accomplish missions ranging from naval diplomacy to enhance national prestige, to SLOC protection, to projection of power ashore from the sea.[46] It is understandable that Korea, whose economy now rates eleventh in the world, wants to possess naval power commensurate with its economic power. However, an arms buildup that goes beyond modernization will create concerns in the region. Therefore, the JMSDF and the ROKN should move in the direction of maintaining their current military structure, supporting a U.S. naval presence in the region as the primary protector of the sea-lanes. The three navies can then cooperate on their future tasks in a supplementary fashion. However, this effort should be done in a way that does not arouse Chinese fear of containment schemes. The Northeast Asian regional multilateral naval CBM, based on the Western Pacific Naval Symposium, for example, should be encouraged to reassure countries in the region.

Multilateral Regional Security Mechanism in Northeast Asia

Engagement of China is a pivotal issue for regional security. China is attempting to prevent U.S. dominance as a hegemonic power and a Japanese military resurgence.[47] Although China has participated in the ASEAN Regional Forum (ARF) since its establishment in 1994, Chinese leadership is suspicious of a multilateral organization.[48] If the United States and Japan initiate the multilateral framework, China will be especially reluctant to join. However, as the reassurance of China is a crucial precondition to developing bilateral Japan–ROK or trilateral U.S.–Japan–ROK defense cooperation, multilateral regional forums to engage and reassure China are required. China recently agreed to hold a second-track trilateral dialogue with the United States and Japan.[49] China is a member of the Northeast Asia Cooperation Dialogue (NEACD), a semigovernmental forum, and the Council for Security Cooperation in the Asian Pacific (CSCAP), a second-track arrangement of ARF. Yet, China seems to skillfully avoid discussing critical security issues in a multilateral setting. However, since there is no time to wait for the natural evolution of an effective multilateral security framework in the region, the United States, Japan, and the ROK should make consistent efforts to engage China through the existing second-track or semigovernmental dialogues.

Nuclear Weapons and Ballistic Missiles

The trigger of the current North Korean problem has been its alleged nuclear weapon production and development of ballistic missiles. Although the North has accepted inspection by the International Atomic Energy Agency (IAEA), the weapons suspicion has not yet been substantiated. Three major nuclear powers—the United States, Russia, and China—have interests in the Korean Peninsula, so denuclearization of the peninsula should be guaranteed by these three nations by having them multilaterally address the North Korean nuclear problem. Though Japan and the ROK are nonnuclear states, both of them rely for their strategic defense on the nuclear umbrella provided by the United States, so they have been automatically involved in the regional nuclear issue whether they like it or not. Japan and the ROK can jointly request the United States to initiate a dialogue among the three nuclear powers regarding denuclearizing the peninsula.

UNPKO

Since both Japan and the ROK are very active in UNPKO, it is worth their effort to join on several types of activities relating to peacekeeping, such as civil engineering projects, medical support, and transportation. In addition, a joint seminar on their respective observations and experiences regarding cease-fire is a possibility. As the main activities of the PKO are usually conducted by ground forces, this provides a good opportunity for interaction; under current conditions, any other direct operational contact of ground forces is still politically difficult, even for the CBM purpose.

Conclusion

Japan and Korea, though direct neighbors, had long been estranged in their defense relationship. Both countries have now been confronted with a potential crisis that affects their common interest. Given the threat posed by North Korea, they have been developing defense cooperation in both bilateral and trilateral (including the United States) fashion. However, the possibility of the demise of the North's threat—whether peacefully or disastrously—having become a real possibility, Japan and the ROK should develop defense cooperation based on a long-term vision. This cooperation between Japan and the ROK, the cornerstone of an overall bilateral bond, should focus first on building confidence and eliminating their legacy of mutual distrust. The cooperation should have long-term goals of reducing uncertainty about the region's future and maintaining regional stability. Whether Japan and Korea will remain as partners or become rivals in the future depends heavily on their defense relationship.

Notes

[1] The author is grateful to Dr. Michael Green of The Council on Foreign Relations for his advice on writing this paper.

[2] Hisahiko Okazaki, *Tonari no Kuni de Kangaeta Koto*, Tokyo Chuo Koron Sham, 1983.

[3] For the scenarios of the future of the Korean Peninsula, see, for example, William Drennan, "Prospects and Implications of Korean Unification," August 22, 1997, Special Report for Policy Forum Online, Northeast Asia Peace and Security Network.

[4] Toshimichi Okubo, a key person in the Meiji Restoration and one of the obligarchs of the Meiji era, called the Korean Peninsula "Japan's line of advantage." It was a consensus among the Japanese that it was necessary to expel Chinese as well as Russian influence, especially in a military sense, from the Korean Peninsula in order to sustain Japan's security.

[5] General Douglas MacArthur, Supreme Commander of the Allied Occupation Forces in Japan, stated before the U.S. Congress that with regard to the Communist threat during the Korean War, that he could understand how Japan's perception that the Korean Peninsula might be dominated by a hostile power could lead to war in the Pacific.

[6] According to an interview by Nicholas Eberstadt with former Deputy Prime Minister Nam Duk Woo in Seoul on September 18, 1984, the ROK political leadership shared the perception that North Korea's general level of development was higher than that of the ROK in the early 1960s. Nicholas Eberstadt, *Korea Approaches Reunification* (Amond, NY: M. E. Sharpe, 1995), p. 13.

[7] Japanese and Korean supporters cheered for each other at the second round of the Asian regional group B qualifier match for the World Cup soccer in Seoul on November 1, which was very unusual. Yomiuri Shimbun, November 4, 1997.

[8] As of November 1997, Japan had participated in four UN peacekeeping operations: UNTAC (Cambodia), ONOUMOZ (Mozambique), UNAMIR II (Rwanda), and UNDOF (Golan Heights).

[9] Japan Defense Agency, *Defense of Japan 1996*, pp. 76, 80.

[10] The new Guidelines for U.S.–Japan Defense Cooperation were agreed to on September 23, 1997, between the U.S. secretaries of defense and state and their Japanese counterparts. The guidelines describe cooperation in three situations: (1) cooperation under normal circumstances, (2) actions in response to an armed attack against Japan, and (3) cooperation in situations in areas surrounding Japan that will have an important influence on Japan's peace and security. For the latter case, the guidelines specified forty items for cooperation, both in activities initiated by either government and Japan's support of U.S. forces activities.

[11] Sang Woo Rhee, "Japan's Role in New Asian Order," *Korea Focus*, May-June, Vol. 4, No. 3 1996, Korea Foundation, p. 27.

[12] The Ministry of National Defense of the ROK, *Defense White Paper* 1991–1992, p. 62. After 1992, the tone of the white paper changed positively by stating, for example that "Japan has been contributing both by direct and indirect means to the peace and security of South Korea," *Defense White Paper* 1992–1993, p. 48.

[13] A report of a workshop "Prospects for U.S.–Korean Naval Relations in 21st Century," held in Seoul on October 17–20, 1994, jointly sponsored by the Center for Naval Analyses and the Korea Institute for Defense Analysis, p. 7.

[14] According to the opinion survey by the government of Japan conducted in February 1997, approximately 70 percent of respondents consider that the U.S.–Japan Security Arrangement contributes to the peace and safety of Japan, and that Japan should secure its defense by a combination of the JSDF and this arrangement.

[15] Japan Defense Agency, *Defense of Japan 1997*, p. 146.

[16] At the Summit of G-7 in 1989, Japan successfully persuaded other member states not to include assertive contemplation of China in the Political Declaration, which was successful. Yomiuri Shimbun, July 15, 1989.

[17] A result of a survey conducted by Yomiuri Shimbun and the Gallup Organization in January and February, 1996, Yomiuri Shimbun, March 17, 1997.

[18] James Cotton, "The Military Factor in South Korean Politics," Viberto Selochan, ed., *The Military, the State, and Development in Asia and the Pacific* (Boulder, Colo.: Westview Press, 1991), pp. 203–220.

[19]Paul Bracken, "The Korean State and Northeast Asia," *Strategic Review*, Summer 1992, p. 43.

[20] The Ministry of National Defense of the ROK, *Defense White Paper* 1996–1997, p.16.

[21] Sang Woo Rhee, "New Defense Posture for Next Century," *Korea Focus on Current Topics*, March-April, Vol. 3, No. 2, 1995, Korea Foundation, p. 61.

[22] *Defense White Paper* cites "(c)onsidering that Korea . . . is the sole nation in the world to hold a truce accord under the supervision of UN forces, its participation in PKO is highly desirable." The Ministry of National Defense of the ROK, *Defense White Paper* 1992–1993, p. 113.

[23] In a ministerial conference on the development of UN peacekeeping forces held on the sidelines of the UN General Assembly, ROK Foreign Minister Chong Ha Yoo pledged that the ROK would an active role in UNPKO. Korea Herald, September 26, 1997.

[24] See, for example, Paul Bracken, op. cit., p. 44, and Yong Ok Park, "Korea's Defense for the 21st Century," *Korea and World Affairs*, Research Center for Peace and Unification of Korea, Vol. XX, No. 1, Spring 1996, p. 23.

[25] The Ministry of National Defense of the ROK, *Defense White Paper* 1996–1997, p. 18.

[26] Seo Hang Lee, "Naval Power as an Instrument of Foreign Policy: The Case of Korea," *Korea Focus on Current Topics*, March-April, Vol. 5, No. 2, 1997, Korea Foundation, p. 33.

[27] *Defense News*, November 25–December 1, 1996.

[28] Don Oberdorfer, *The Two Koreas* (Reading: Addison-Wesley, 1997), pp. 5–6.

[29] See, for example, the report of a workshop "Trilateral Naval Cooperation: Japan–U.S.–Korea," in Tokyo on February 13–14, 1997, jointly sponsored by The Center for Naval Analyses, Korea Institute for Defense Analyses, and the National Institute for Defense Studies, p. 16.

[30] *Korea Herald*, September 13, 1997. See also an opinion survey, sponsored by the USIA and conducted in June 1996, that shows that 75 percent of respondents do not see a need for U.S. forces to stay in Korea after reunification and 70 percent think the best way to ensure Korea's future security is to strengthen its own defense capability and defend itself. "Security Ties," *Pacific Bridge*, Winter 1996, Vol. 5, No. 4, The Korea-America Friendship Society, p. 6.

[31] The Ministry of National Defense of the ROK, *Defense White Paper* 1996, p. 137.

[32] Fei Ling Wang, "Chinese Perception of the U.S.–ROK Alliance," a paper presented to the International Workshop on the U.S.–ROK Alliance, Seoul, Korea, October 5–7, 1995, Nautilus, Online.

[33] Ibid.

[34] This is a result of the author's interviews with a high-ranking ROK defense official, scholars close to the ROK Ministry of National Defense, and ROK military officers.

[35] For example, see, The Ministry of National Defense of the ROK, *Defense White Paper* 1996–1997, pp. 44–46.

[36] Don Oberdorfer, op. cit., p. 409.

[37] See Robert Dujarric, *Korean Unification and After* (Hudson, 2000).

[38] Michael Green, "U.S.–Japan–ROK Trilateral Security Cooperation," an unpublished conference paper presented at the annual meeting of the American Political Science Association, Washington, D.C., on August 28–30, 1997, p. 2.

[39] Statement of a high-ranking JSDF officer in an interview with the author.

[40] These issues are articulated by the author as a result of discussions with both U.S. and South Korean civilian officials, military officers, and scholars.

[41] These activities are articulated by the author based on the agreed CBM at the fifth West Pacific Naval Symposium (WPNS) held in Tokyo in November 1996, in which top naval officers from 18 countries participated, including Japan, the United States, the ROK, Russia, and China.

[42] Japan Defense Agency, *Defense of Japan 1997*, pp. 98–100.

[43] Michael Green, op. cit., p. 13.

[44] Ibid., p. 4, and The Ministry of National Defense of the ROK, *Defense White Paper* 1996–1997, p. 137.

[45] Japan Defense Agency, *Defense of Japan 1997*, p. 103.

[46] Report of a workshop, "Naval Cooperation After Korean Unification," held in Washington, D.C., December 4–5, 1995, jointly sponsored by The Center of Naval Analyses and the Korea Institute for Defense Analyses, pp. 12–13.

[47] Fei Ling Wang, op. cit.

[48] Thomas Christensen, "Chinese Realpolitik," *Foreign Affairs*, September-October, 1996, pp. 38–39.

[49] Yomiuri Shimbun, November 1, 1997.

Searching for a Korean-Japanese Strategic Partnership:

Beyond Maritime Confidence Building Measures

By Akihisa Nagashima

A paper prepared for the 6th Korea-Japan Shuttle for Maritime Cooperation
Etajima, Japan
June 13–17, 1998

Introduction

Ever since reading a book entitled *Tonari no kuni de kangaeta koto* (What I Thought in a Neighboring Country, Korea), by Ambassador Okazaki Hisahiko,[1] I have been profoundly interested in someday seeing full reconciliation between Japan and Korea. My most recent experience with Korean affairs at the Council on Foreign Relations (CFR) further convinced me of the growing urgency of improving relations across the Tsushima Strait. I recently worked on an Independent Task Force on Korea sponsored by the CFR. Throughout the eight months of meetings attended by all former assistant secretaries of state and U.S. ambassadors to Seoul since the Reagan administration as well as by prominent Korea and Asia experts from various think tanks, the troubled history of the Republic of Korea (ROK)–Japanese relations greatly concerned the participants.[2] It was frequently stated at the meetings that Japan fears the reunification of the Korean Peninsula and that there is little chance for U.S.–ROK–Japanese defense planners to discuss contingency cooperation because some activities of the Japan Self-Defense Forces (JSDF) may involve Korean territories, and so forth. It is true that the U.S–ROK–Japan trilateral policy coordination with regard to the Korean Peninsula, albeit recognized as desirable, is always hampered by the difficult history of Japan-Korea relations.[3]

This paper attempts to redefine Japan-Korea relations from the strategic point of view; it will explore various maritime cooperation options as a basis for a solid bilateral partnership in the somewhat fluid environment of Northeast Asia, transcending the troubled history between the two countries. The paper will finally propose three policy recommendations, primarily to the Japanese government, for achieving the objective of building a strategic partnership between Japan and Korea.

The Missing "Leg" of the Triangle

In dealing with the Northeast Asian geostrategic dynamics, especially in the long run, the status of the Korea-Japan bilateral relationship is particularly frustrating. In coping with change on the Korean Peninsula, for example, this fatally weak leg in the American security triangle has made it more difficult to deal with a wide range of issues including KEDO coordination, food aid, normalization with North Korea, and financial assistance. Although both the U.S.–Japan alliance and the U.S.–ROK alliance have been actively maintained throughout *and* well beyond the Cold War, the other leg of that triangle has never been actively connected. Indeed, a typical conclusion from a series of first- and second-track dialogues between the United States, Japan, and the ROK states that "Korea domestic politics will limit trilateral cooperation, as will emotional issues linked to the past and divergent views on the historical record. Limitations on expanded military operations, established in Japan's constitution, will also constrain cooperation."[4]

But the time has finally come for the Koreans and Japanese alike to take a bolder step toward a historic reconciliation between the two neighboring countries. Three trends suggest that there is a new opportunity to do this.

First, the new President of the ROK, Kim Dae Jung, dared to unveil his "sunshine" policy toward Japan as well as North Korea. In his inaugural speech, President Kim articulated his intention to improve relations with Japan; one of the first acts of his administration was the gradual elimination of a ban on cultural inflow from Japan. President Kim also publicly stated that he was willing to invite the Japanese Emperor to Korea for the first time in history. The recent local election victory of his ruling coalition is an encouraging event that would further strengthen Kim's political base. Further, President Kim's first state visit to Japan, which took place in October 1998, will provided an invaluable opportunity to begin a totally new relationship and overcome the troubled past.

Second, the prolonged and uncertain situation in the North has been providing, ironically, a golden opportunity for Seoul and Tokyo to work together on a wide range of issues, from economics to security. Given the potential threat posed by North Korea either by its explosion or implosion, Japan and South Korea, with support and encouragement from the United States, have continued to improve bilateral consultation and cooperation on security issues even in the midst of serious controversy over the fisheries agreement and the territorial disputes over Takeshima/Tokdo. However, once the North Korean threat dissipates, there may be new security challenges that are considerably less obvious than the present one. The ROK government, therefore, is now searching for a future-oriented defense policy focused on regional stability rather than on simply maintaining deterrence of North Korea.[5] In this context, according to recent news reports, the ROK and the United States are currently considering how the 1953 ROK–U.S. Mutual Defense Treaty can be used to take into account the current status of their alliance. The focus of the treaty would be shifted from coping with the North Korean threat to "cooperation between the two countries for peace and stability in northeast Asia and the Asia-Pacific region." [6]

Third, events on the Japanese security policy front since the embarrassing failure during the 1991 Gulf War could pave the way for the Japanese to take a more realistic and proactive approach to national security and international relations in the post–Cold War era.[7] For example, the 1997 U.S.–Japan Defense Guidelines and their implementation process have virtually marginalized the long-standing Japanese debate over the right of collective self-defense. Most Japanese activities included in the rear-area support for U.S. forces (which, during the Gulf War, were considered to be *unconstitutional* because they exceeded the minimum needed for self-defense) became *constitutional* as the so-called gray areas were cleared away in the process. Minesweeping during the conflict, maritime interdiction operations under the auspices of the UN, and the contingency ACSA (as well as the peacetime one), all once included in the gray area, are now allowed. As a result, there seems to be a certain consensus, albeit still implicit, among Japanese leadership ranging from Nakasone Yasuhiro (known to be hawkish on national security) to Miyazawa Kiichi (known to be dovish) that the defensive operations of JSDF with U.S. forces outside the territory of Japan should be constitutional as long as there is no combat by the JSDF in third countries.[8] In addition, the JSDF's overseas operations have become quite common since it was dispatched in 1993 to participate in U.S. peacekeeping operations in Cambodia as well as in noncombatant evacuation operations vis-à-vis Cambodia in 1997 and Indonesia in 1998. The supporting legislation for those operations has recently been improved. More important, bilateral military exercises in search and rescue with Russia in July 1998 were the first-ever bilateral exercises with a state other than the United States, and amazingly, no opposition parties have publicly criticized this decision. The need to cope with the uncertain strategic environment of the post–Cold War in general, and the recent currency crisis surrounding Japan in particular, is moving the Japanese toward a more realistic and practical security policy.

Naval Cooperation for Building a Strategic Partnership

Recent years in Northeast Asia have witnessed a symbolic restructuring of the power equation in the post–Cold War era. China and Russia elevated their relationship from a "constructive" to a "strategic partnership" in 1996. The United States and China declared themselves on similar terms, leaving behind their historical difficulties and differences in values, and stressing instead the geostrategic significance of their relationships. Korean-Japanese relations should also confirm the notion of a strategic partnership in the sense that the direction and closeness of the bilateral relationship will have a significant strategic impact on the environment of northeast Asia. In this regard, one of the most profound conclusions from a series of K-J Shuttle meetings and U.S.–Japan–ROK trilateral conferences organized by the Okazaki Institute is that the key concept of a prospective Japan-Korea "strategic partnership" should be built based upon maritime cooperation. A maritime coalition, if not alliance, between Japan and Korea would be able to deal with a variety of future scenarios in the region. It would be a workable partnership for three reasons:

First, it is hard to imagine that Japan-Korea bilateral cooperation would involve Japanese ground forces, because of historical as well as operational considerations. In a crisis on the Korean Peninsula, for example, for the new U.S.–Japan Defense Guidelines to be effective, possible ROK–Japan cooperation with U.S. forces would include noncombatant evacuation operations, intelligence sharing, search and rescue, maritime interdiction operations, and so forth.[9] These are primarily maritime missions.[10]

Second, in the foreseeable future, Japan and Korea would be expected to provide no more than "assistance projection" capabilities to complement U.S. power-projection capabilities.[11]

Third, Korean and Japanese common national interests rely heavily on maritime security, given the phenomenal trade-driven nature of the two countries. Freedom of navigation is crucial for both and would provide an impetus for bilateral security cooperation such as protection of sea lines of communication (SLOCs).[12]

Impact of Strategic Maritime Cooperation

The focal issue of the strategic dynamics in the Asia-Pacific region for at least the first quarter of the twenty-first century would involve the United States and China: hegemonic power versus emerging power. China's strategic objective, on the one hand, is to expand its sphere of influence as much as possible, while maintaining a stable surrounding environment (with the exception of the Taiwan case) to sustain its long-range economic growth. On the other hand, the U.S. strategic objective is to maintain the status quo global order with a resilient web of alliances as long as possible, at a cost as low as possible. In this context, Japan and Korea hold a significant strategic position. If Korea, surrounded by powerful Asian neighbors, aligns itself with China against Japan and the United States, the consequences would be rather tragic: a classical geopolitical example of "land power versus maritime power" confrontation. The key factor in avoiding such polarity is whether Japan and Korea can collaborate effectively, based on their current set of security arrangements with the United States, to create a solid foundation for China to integrate fully into the international order. And the concept of maritime cooperation posits these two alliances having overlapping security interests. In sum, the distance between Japan and Korea would determine the viability of *smaller* triangle relations between the United States, Japan, and the ROK, as well as the stability of *larger* triangle relations between China, the United States, and Asia as a whole.

Meanwhile, ongoing U.S.–Japan–ROK trilateral consultative forums with the policy-planning staffs are expected to allow Japan and South Korea to discuss long-term U.S. defense commitments in the region.[13] A robust U.S. military presence as a crucial stabilizing factor in the region is essential to both countries' security policy formulations. In addition, U.S. engagement would provide the most reliable basis for strengthening Japan–ROK mutual confidence. Moreover, a common U.S.–ROK–Japan agreement on a long-term U.S. presence would put the relations of all three nations with China on a solid footing, given the expectation that growing Chinese criticism of a U.S. presence is a critical destabilizing factor in the region. Cohosting of the U.S. presence by Japan and Korea, if necessary for budgetary and political reasons, may be worth considering in light of the expected reorganization of the U.S. forward-deployed force structure, which will take place after the end of the North Korean menace.

However, some wild cards persist that may hinder Korean and Japanese security policy and military personnel. On the one hand, the fact that Tokyo's security policy has already departed from mere home defense and that its security role will inevitably expand as its security interests and threats are diversified is likely to concern Seoul, given Korea's historic distrust of Japan. On the other hand, Japanese defense officials reportedly express concern[14] that the ROK government has pursued a more ambitious defense policy, shifting from its concentration on ROK Army deterrence of aggression by the North; acquiring submarines from Germany in 1987 and P-3C maritime patrol aircraft from the United States in 1990; and starting indigenous production of submarines and KDX destroyers and licensed production of F-16 fighters.[15]

Importance of an Operational Focus

Despite all the concerns regarding the necessity for operational levels of military cooperation as well as close policy coordination between Tokyo and Seoul, the current focus seems to be on mere confidence-building measures (CBMs), originally designed to avoid actual military engagement between enemies, namely the United States and the Soviet Union. My graduate research project was to explore the possibility of creating a "Standing Naval Force" in the Asia-Pacific region with the United States and China under a single authority. This admittedly ambitious work was aimed at studying various Multinational Naval Cooperation Options (MNCOs) among all nations in the region as potentially important tools for deepening regional cooperative security. My motivation was to explore how we might develop effective security mechanisms to counter possible regional crises, transcending the current efforts of CBMs in the region. I felt pessimistic about the mere continuation of dialogue and personnel exchanges between military forces in the region, while not discounting the significance of such measures among states that do not trust each other.

Through a review of historical experience and various studies and proposals by scholars and military experts, the research first identifies and discusses possible MNCOs ranging from CBMs to more ambitious missions or combat operations. Second, the research examines options for organizing and managing the desired MNCOs in view of (1) the nature of authority needed for multinational naval cooperation (MNC), (2) the problem of command and control of the participating forces, and (3) the process of developing the cooperation in accordance with regional characteristics. Finally, the paper makes some suggestions for U.S. and Japanese roles in an institutionalized MNC charged with building cooperative security mechanisms in the region.

The conclusion of my research was that the mission focus of MNC in the region tends to depend on the following three conditions:

- low political risks (i.e., nonpartisan)
- lower-intensity end of missions
- less demanding technical requirements

Those mission focuses of MNC that met with the preceding conditions, as shown in Figures 1 and 2, include search and rescue (SAR), disaster relief and humanitarian assistance, constabulary mission/piracy suppression, peacekeeping (category 1), and when the situation allows, maritime interdiction operations (MIO), noncombatant evacuation operations (NEO), and mine-countermeasures (category 2).

In Asia, some afloat naval cooperation missions have been instrumental in building the region's confidence. In fact, the 1996 WPNS included the first two measures—notably, "relief activities in large-scale disasters" and "SAR operation and training" in its agenda for maritime CBMs. In general, the first and second categories, due to their low-key nature, could be an objective of institutionalized MNC in the Asia-Pacific region, where states do not necessarily share their threat perceptions. Specifically, the first four missions in category 1 require the least political involvement. Exercises and actual operations of the first category, therefore, can be conducted without interruption in such a way that the missions can be tested through actual operations immediately after the exercises. Moreover, those mission-focused exercises and operations appear to have progressed in the region without alarming neighboring countries that do not take part in the cooperative efforts. By contrast, missions in the third category (and the second one to a certain extent) require a potential target (or adversary), and thus an actual operation never occurs unless a contingency event takes place. The third category of combat operations, therefore, may thus be suited only to an alliance or ad hoc coalition resulting from a compelling need to meet aggression or apparent threats.

Figure 1. Prospective Afloat Naval Cooperation Mission Spectrum

Mission Focus		Examples (Exercise/Operation)
Low-intensity end		
• Search and rescue (SAR)	⇒	Joint Malaysia-Singapore SAREX
• Disaster relief/Humanitarian assistance	⇒	Operation *Sea Angel* (in Bangladesh)/ Somalia (UNOSOM), *Cooperation from the Sea* (U.S.–Russia)
• Constabulary mission/Piracy suppression	⇒	Joint Patrol Fleet of the Thai-Malaysian Sea Borders
• Peacekeeping	⇒	ONUCA (in Nicaragua), UNTAC (in Cambodia)
Higher-intensity end		
• Peace enforcement/Embargo enforcement	⇒	Beira patrol (UK), Gulf/Red Sea (ad hoc coalition), Adriatic (WEU/NATO)
• Noncombatant evacuation operations (NEO)	⇒	Yemen (UK), Liberia, Somalia (US)
• Coastal defense/Mine countermeasures (MCM)	⇒	Korean War, Iran-Iraq War, Gulf War
Combat operation		
• Air-defense/Anti-submarine warfare (ASW)	⇒	Major ADEX (FPDA) / RIMPAC
• Amphibious assault	⇒	Joint-Combined Exercises *Kangaroo*, *Team Spirit*, *Cobra Gold*

Figure 2. Functions of Potential Naval Cooperation Options

		Functions
Low-intensity end		
• Search and rescue (SAR)	⇒	Almost no risk of conflict, no threat to peace, equivalent to a traditional peacekeeping
• Disaster relief/Humanitarian assistance	⇒	Disaster relief operations are same as above
• Constabulary mission/Piracy suppression	⇒	Humanitarian intervention to protect or rescue victims of conflict risks participation in war
• Peacekeeping	⇒	Postwar mine clearing, piracy suppression, safety surveillance for shipping, suppression of smuggling (of arms, drugs, animals, and artifacts), pollution control, hydrographic surveys, and policing of ocean conservation agreements
	⇒	Support task for land-based peacekeeping forces, which include logistic and C4I support to and integration with land-based operations; monitor and observe cease-fire; and establish disengagement zones
Higher-intensity end		
• Peace enforcement/Embargo enforcement	⇒	The deployment of naval power to deter aggression; to coerce, break, or establish blockades; or engage in combat with the purpose of upholding international law or enforcing UN rulings (Ch. VII of UN Charter)
• Noncombatant evacuation operations (NEO)	⇒	Transit protection, escorts through minefields and the defense of shipping in war zones
• Mine countermeasures (MCM)	⇒	Removing threatened civilian noncombatants (including refugees and in rare cases, combatants) from locations abroad
	⇒	Primarily humanitarian in nature but may have military implications
	⇒	Mine-clearing, not only post-conflict

Beginning with Training and Exercises

As a consequence, I proposed in my graduate research project that a Standing Naval Force Pacific–Training (STANAVFORPAC–Training) be launched, using naval units earmarked by member states and running regularly scheduled joint exercises. This would be under the supervision of a single authoritative organization, consisting of force commanders and planning officers representing each member state and having rotating responsibilities.[16] Benefits of the exercise in the context of confidence building include:

- higher preparedness for actual operations
- thoroughly transparent CBMs
- a reliable basis for nurturing a "partnership"

Militarily speaking, exercises and training ought to be designed to serve actual operations. But naval exercises have frequently been referred to in the context of CBMs among states. Combined exercises are bound to enhance personnel exchanges and the inter-operability of communication systems, weapon technology, and some degree of operational doctrine. Furthermore, these personnel exchanges will achieve a far more significant level of transparency than will those by informational measures, such as the publication of the *Defense White Paper*. Multinational exercises, as Admiral Owens suggested, will also optimize military-to-military and political-to-political contacts and will raise not only preparedness for coalition warfare but also political effectiveness in contingencies. Such multinational interactions might further require participating states and their forces to create Standard Operating Procedures (SOPs) and develop standardized weapon systems and even to agree to study joint procurement. These effects would not only act as CBMs to reduce tensions but would also bind new partners closer together.

A good example of cooperation in military efforts is the Integrated Air-Defense System (IADS) shared by Malaysia and Singapore and sharpened through periodic combined exercises between the two air forces under the FPDA. It has played a remarkable role since 1971 in preventing the two nations from entering into confrontation and in defending the Malay Peninsula itself, providing a stable environment around the strategic choke point of the Straits of Malacca.[17]

Other precedents of naval cooperation among ASEAN countries in a wide range of missions are inspiring and encouraging to us. Moreover, most of the combined naval exercises and operations are bilateral and well developed, with each country taking turns hosting them in its own waters. Some of these precedents are described as follows:

Indonesia and Singapore have been conducting cooperative antipiracy patrols since 1993. These exercises are scheduled quarterly and consist of a tactical gaming exercise and two months of coordinated patrols. The ASEAN regional forum (ARF) is already embarked on discussing the creation of a training center for peacekeeping operations.[18]

As for SAR, Singapore, Malaysia, and Indonesia have developed Joint SAREX on a bilateral basis, and the recent ARF Intercession Meeting on SAR chaired by the United States and Singapore witnessed ARF members agreeing to the publication of a directory of regional SAR contact points as well as looking into various areas of SAR cooperation.[19]

As for constabulary missions, Malaysia has established a Joint Maritime Action Program, the OPTIMA and PHIMA, with Indonesia and the Philippines, respectively, to deal with criminal activities along their common sea boundaries.[20] An agreement was made with Malaysia to form a joint force, called the Joint Fleet of the Thai-Malaysian Sea Borders, to patrol the two countries' adjacent territorial waters. In addition, the patrol fleet conducts a combined exercise code-named SEAEX THAMAL, and they drill periodically to establish standard operating procedures.[21]

These findings, I believe, would provide some useful suggestions for us in considering naval cooperation options involving Japan and the ROK. Meanwhile, since the nature of operations will compel participating forces to enter into territorial waters, missions in the second category—albeit essentially lower-intensity—remain politically sensitive. Nevertheless, as operations with regard to Bosnia, Somalia, Haiti, and Liberia have demonstrated, these measures are increasingly important to contain a post–Cold War threat and to protect citizens and ensure that the freedom of navigation is not affected by the threat. These points, therefore, prompt us to consider what the mission focus should be for Japan-Korea maritime cooperation, and what obstacles should be removed to *upgrade* prospective activities from the low-intensity first category to the more politically sensitive second category.

Conclusion: Create History, Shape the Future

Unless Japan and the ROK successfully ease the distrust among their respective peoples, emotional domestic politics will most likely continue to be a significant destabilizing factor for the bilateral relationship, let alone upgrade it to a "strategic partnership." The Japanese have often made the argument that "no one can quickly resolve the troubled history that lies between Japan and Korea, and we should instead expect future leaders of both countries to solve it eventually." I disagree strongly with this kind of resignation among Japanese! How can we just wait for another decade or so before tackling the core of problems that exists between the two countries, despite the fact that both sides recognize the growing urgency of reconciliation? In other words, maritime cooperation is the key to building a strategic partnership between Japan and Korea, but this is only one level of effort. Larger issues must be simultaneously addressed.

To conclude, I would like to present three policy recommendations for breaking the ice between Japan and Korea. Needless to say, my proposals, which mainly address Japanese efforts, do not preclude sincere efforts on the Korean side in response to Japanese actions, such as easing excessively antagonistic expressions against Japan in Korean school textbooks and treating fairly the pro-Japanese reform movement, led by Kim Ok-kyun in the 1880s, to jointly remove the thorns of their regrettable past.

Three major thorns to be removed are (1) the grievance over "comfort women," a symbol of Imperial Japan's brutal occupation of Korea, (2) wartime liabilities, frequently whitewashed by Japanese ultraconservative politicians, and (3) territorial disputes over Takeshima/Tokdo, overshadowing every single Japanese proactive move in security areas. And my aim is to create "moral high ground," as President Kim has done since his election in December 1997, vis-à-vis the reconciliation of the two countries.

First, there should be thorough and comprehensive disclosures of official information regarding "comfort women," allegedly still classified within the National Police Agency, Defense Agency, and Home Affairs Ministry,[22] so that the Japanese public becomes fully aware of what is "true," as well as enabling all registered victims in Korea and elsewhere to bring their cases to Japanese courts and get proper *personal* compensation from the government of Japan if need be.

Second, every cabinet should enact a resolution, or *kakugi-kettei,* at its initial meeting to require members of the cabinet to commit themselves to withholding their personal opinions regarding the "interpretation of history," so that no one in the cabinet would deviate from the official line while in office and confuse Japanese foreign policy to the detriment of the national interest.

Third, the government of Japan should unilaterally declare that Japan's territorial claim over Takeshima be put aside. It should call for promptly convening a bilateral commission to discuss a "new border" between Japan and Korea and propose that Japan and Korea jointly revert to the so-called Peace Line, based on the MacArthur Line of 1946, which separates Japanese and Korean sea space at a point equidistant between the outskirts of the territories of the two countries, where Takeshima/Tokdo barely falls into Korean territorial waters.

Let me elaborate a bit on each of those proposals. First, we all are aware that the "comfort women" issue is the heart of Korean *han,* or feeling of regret and repulsion. But fundamental problems lie in the inordinate lack of information. According to Professor Yoshimi Yoshiaki of Chuo University, who discovered new information that prompted the Miyazawa government to accept the state's responsibility for having organized comfort women and led Kono Yohei, then the cabinet's chief secretary, to issue a formal apology in August 1993, there is still a considerable amount of classified information within the related ministries of Japan. As you might assume, at the time the National Police Agency had issued passports for women sent to frontlines stretching across Asia; however, that has remained classified. The Home Affairs Ministry is supposed to hold a significant amount of information because it partly succeeded the Interior Ministry, which controlled the governor-generals of Korea and Taiwan in the prewar period. In addition, thousands of administrative journals and war diaries are believed to be held in the National Institute for Defense Studies of the Defense Agency, but only hundreds have been declassified so far. As a result, most Japanese unfortunately are unaware of what really happened and of the real role of the government with regard to "comfort women" during wartime, except for a variety of "interpretations" and the agitation maximized by ideologically biased activists and scholars in Japan.

Second, we are all irritated that after each formal apology made by the emperors, prime ministers, and others of the Japanese leadership, some cabinet member, one of only twenty-two political leaders of Japan, makes astonishingly inappropriate remarks on his personal "interpretation of history." These remarks have ruined constructive political leadership in Japan quite effectively. In order for Japan to maintain a consistent foreign policy, we should stop this vicious circle by effective and authoritative measures. Germany, for example, has legislation to limit cabinet members' remarks on Nazism. Needless to say, of course, we should not constrain any person's freedom of speech, including a politician's right to express his or her "interpretation of history."

Third, as for Takeshima/Tokdo, we all know that there is more than ample evidence that each side has claimed to support its arguments, dating back to the sixth century. But according to "facts" neither Koreans nor Japanese can deny, Japan's unilateral declaration of its sovereignty over Takeshima was made in January 1905, in the middle of the Russo-Japanese War, but the notification to Korea was not made until 1906, after Japan deprived Korea of diplomatic and military authority by the Second Japan-Korea Agreement or by the Eulsa Treaty of November 1905. Then, as we all know, the ratification of the Eulsa Treaty was forced by the Japanese delegation led by Ito Hirobumi and General Hasegawa, and there were no signatures by the king and the prime minister of Korea. That is why the Takeshima/Tokdo issue always angers the Koreans, whereas the Japanese government maintains that their claim is supported by international law.

As Professor Lee Chong-Sik underscores, "Korea's approach to Japan was spiritual, moral, holistic, and Oriental, whereas the Japanese approach was legalistic, pragmatic, piecemeal, and Western."[23] We should explore a "new thinking" based more on the former approach, a moral one, yet still within the middle ground of both sides. In my view, the Peace Line happens to provide an ideal middle ground for both. Suppose that there is no Takeshima/Tokdo, and then draw the line at a point equidistant between territories of Japan and Korea, i.e., between Ulung-do and Oki-shima, which happens to be the same as the Peace Line. That is, Japan does not have to drop its territorial claim over Takeshima, but will still yield these islets to Korea. Korea does not have to abandon its effective control over Tokdo, but instead sets back its Exclusive Economic Zone (EEZ) to the line so both can find a real fisheries agreement that allows both countries to operate jointly within the certain zone or exclusively within each EEZ.[24] The bottom line here is to contain the Takeshima/Tokdo issue within purely economic and fishing concerns of the two countries. In sum, this is the only way that Koreans can keep their "actual" control over Tokdo, while the Japanese keep their "virtual" sovereignty over Takeshima. More important, we should contain the so-called "history card" to prevent it from being used in diplomatic and security dialogue, which would directly affect other troubled relations: those with China. The very point here is to create a "moral high ground" vis-à-vis Korea and other neighbors, so that Japan could strengthen its fundamental strategic posture, "shin" in the Sun Zhu's terminology, as quickly and solidly as possible.

As a matter of course, the preceding proposals would stir up a lot of other side-effect problems. For example, (1) the disclosure of critical information would open the debate over the state compensation issue that both governments officially declared to be solved in 1965; (2) the fact that Japan has to take forceful measures to restrain cabinet members' freedom of expression might be seen by others as revealing how weak Japanese public consensus is; and (3) Japan should think about policy consistency with other border dispute cases such as those with Russia and China, and so forth. Former Prime Minister Nakasone Yasuhiro, for example, and a Korean equivalent, a respected progressive conservative political leader might chair a Bilateral Reconciliation Commission, talking freely about Takeshima/Tokdo, expressions of each country's textbooks, comfort women issues, and other remaining problems, based on the proposals. But in this regard we should remember that President Nixon was furiously attacked by both conservatives and human rights activists when he made a historic rapprochement with China in 1972, and Beijing made a bold decision to normalize its relations with Seoul at the risk of "blood ties" with Pyongyang in 1992.

I have long been pondering and discussing with Korean friends what Japan and Korea should and can do for this historic reconciliation to take place. These three recommendations are my conclusions to date. These should not necessarily be carried out at the same time, and instead, an incremental approach would be more promising, but we should not put off the critical decision making any longer. In addition, "conservatives," I believe, have a primary responsibility to break through the stalemate stemming from the "burden of history," just as a conservative Richard Nixon made a historic rapprochement with Communist China and, although on a much lower scale, an ultra-leftist Murayama Tomiichi embraced the SDF, the U.S.–Japan security alliance, Hinomaru (the Japanese flag), and Kimigayo (the national anthem of Japan).

Notes

[1] Okazaki Hisahiko, *Tonari no kuni de kangaeta koto* [What I Thought in a Neighboring Country, Korea] (Tokyo: Chuo Koron, 1983).

[2] The report of this project entitled "An Independent Task Force on Managing Change on the Korean Peninsula Sponsored by The Council on Foreign Relations," has just been published by The Council on Foreign Relations, Inc. (New York, 1998).

[3] See, for example, Michael J. Green, "U.S.–Japan–ROK Trilateral Security Cooperation: Prospects and Pitfalls," a paper prepared for the annual meeting of the American Political Science Association (Washington, D.C.: August 28–31, 1997). See also RADM Kawamura Sumihiko (JMSDF, Ret.), "Trilateral Cooperation for Assistance Projection," a paper prepared for the 1998 Japan-Korea–U.S. Trilateral Naval Cooperation Workshop (Hawaii, May 14–15, 1998), p. 1.

[4] A Workshop Report on "Trilateral Naval Cooperation: Japan–U.S.–Korea" Sponsored by the Center for Naval Analyses, Korea Institute for Defense Analyses, and National Institute for Defense Studies (Tokyo, February 13–14, 1997) p. 33.

[5] The Ministry of National Defense of the Republic of Korea, *Defense White Paper* 1996–1997 (Seoul, 1997),p. 18.

[6] *Seoul Shimun* (May 30, 1998). The article goes on to say that "the source said that the new treaty would contain provisions for a continued U.S. military presence in Korea after the peninsula's reunification. Bearing in mind the new U.S.–Japan Defense Guidelines, the source reported that a potential ROK–Japanese security cooperation agreement is also under consideration."

[7] For more details, see Nagashima Akihisa, "Futsu no kuni ni motomerareru seiji no shinryo: Anzen-hosho big bang seikou eno michi" [Political Prudence Is Needed in a "Normal State": Keys to Success for Japanese "Security Big Bang,"] in *Anzen-hosho no big bang* [Security Big Bang] (Tokyo: Yomiuri Shimbun-sha, 1998) pp. 9–37.

[8] Nagashima Akihisa, "Saying Sayonara to the Barren Debate on Collective Defense," *Japan Digest* (September 25, 1997) p. 5.

[9] For details, see The Okazaki Institute/Ogawa Akira, "Simulation: A Contingency on the Korean Peninsula, How the U.S. and Japan Move According to the New Guidelines," The Okazaki Institute website: www.glocomnet.or.jp/okazaki-inst/glsimu.html.

[10] Of course, there would be activities conducted by the JASDF and the JGSDF in the event of Korean contingency.

[11] The phrase "assistance projection" was coined by a participant in the first trilateral naval cooperation workshop held in Tokyo in February 1997. See a Workshop Report on "Trilateral Naval Cooperation: Japan–U.S.–Korea," Sponsored by the Center for Naval Analyses, Korea Institute for Defense Analyses, and National Institute for Defense Studies (Tokyo, February 13–14, 1997) pp. 18–19.

[12] Yun Dokmin specifically emphasizes ROK–Japan cooperation for SLOC defense in his striking article entitled "Kan-nichi ampo wo kangaeru toki" [The Time Has Come to Consider Korea-Japan Security Cooperation], *This Is Yomiuri* (December 1996) pp. 197–198.

[13] Michael J. Green, "Japan and the Future of the Korean Peninsula," a paper prepared for the Association of Asian Studies Annual Meeting (Washington, D.C.: March 18–25, 1998).

[14] *Defense News* (November 25–December 1, 1996).

[15] Seo Hang Lee, "Naval Power as an Instrument of Foreign Policy: The Case of Korea," *Korea Focus on Current Topics*, 5:2 (March-April, 1997) p. 33.

[16] Remember that my assumption then included the United States and China under a single authoritative organization that manages the multinational naval cooperation in the entire region. The issue of command structure of the multinational exercise regime was discussed in my research paper: "Standing Naval Force Pacific: A Key to an Asia-Pacific Security Community" (Washington, D.C.: The Paul H. Nitze School of Advanced International Studies, December 1996).

[17] Western Pacific Naval Experts at the Fifth Western Pacific Naval Symposium, An Evaluation and Proposal on Maritime Confidence-Building Measures (Tokyo: Japan Maritime Defense Force, November 27, 1996).

[18] Pengiran Osman Bin Pengiran Haji Patra, "The Future Course of the ASEAN Regional Forum: Openness and the Regional Approach to Disarmament," *Disarmament,* 18-2 (1995): pp. 145–157.

[19] Col. Lui Tuck Yew, RSN, "Alternate Perspectives on Naval Cooperation," a paper prepared for CSCAP Working Group on Maritime Cooperation (Kuala Lumpur, April 16–17, 1996).

[20] Ltd. Cdr. Razali Md. Ali, "Naval Cooperation: The Malaysian Perspective," CSCAP, op.cit.

[21] VADM Nitz Srisomwong, "Regional Naval Cooperation," CSCAP, op. cit.

[22] Yoshimi Yoshiaki, "State's Crime Should Be Compensated by State," *Asahi Shimbun* (August 22, 1995) p. 18.

[23] Chung-Sik Lee, *Japan and Korea: The Political Dimension* (California: Stanford University Hoover Institution Press, 1985) pp. 24–25.

[24] The author recognizes the current negotiation process between Japanese and Korean governments to strike a new fisheries agreement after Japan's unilateral termination of the current agreements on January 23, 1998. Japan and the ROK established their EEZ in July 1996, but they have not applied it to the sea space between the two countries since the current agreement has been effective (and will be effective until January 1999). The two governments are holding a series of dialogues to establish (1) a "temporary zone of joint operation" around the disputed Takeshima/Tokdo, the scope of which Tokyo and Seoul fell short of the accord in January 1998; (2) a fishing quota derived from TAC which Japanese government imposed on its own fishermen strictly since 1997; and (3) self-restraint measures on the outskirts of each territorial waters, but have not reached any agreement yet. Unless the two governments strike the "new deal" by January 1999, however, they might have to apply two hundred nautical miles of EEZ to the sea space between Japan and Korea, where the territorial dispute over Takeshima/Tokdo will again arise as a central issue between the two countries.

Japan and the Korean Peninsula:

The Economy of South Korea and Economic Cooperation After Unification

By Hattori Tamio,
Professor, Comparative Sociology at
Doshisha University in Kyoto

Economic Difficulties Confronting South Korea

Since the summer of 1997, South Korea has been faced with a seriously deteriorating economic environment. Korea's exports have been in the doldrums, and a series of management crises have beset the medium-sized *chaebol* groups (*zaibatsu* in Japanese, or conglomerates). In the summer of 1997, even the eighth-largest group in terms of assets, the Kia Group, was in crisis, and the situation worsened when the decision on provisional quasi-nationalization[1] of the group was delayed. Furthermore, the sixth-largest group, the Sunkyong Group, sold an affiliated paper-manufacturing company and was seeking a buyer for its auto manufacturer. (The fourth-largest group, the Daewoo Group, decided on the acquisition.) The twelfth-largest group, the Hanjin Group, began extensive employee layoffs (before its bankruptcy on December 6, 1997), and rumors of financial crises have spread to the medium-sized Hai Tae Group as well. In addition, the fourth- and eighth-largest firms in the securities industry have declared bankruptcy.

The business difficulties of these corporations are the tip of the iceberg. Management difficulties resulting from the rapid increase in loans extended by financial institutions that are now not recoverable seem to have stabilized temporarily because of financial support from the government, but the stock market, with the uncertain future of South Korea's economy, has declined significantly. The overall index, which exceeded 1,000 around the end of 1994, accelerated its decline after the summer of 1997 and fell to below 400 by the end of November. The decline since then has been particularly rapid.

Both the domestic and foreign environments enveloping the South Korean economy deteriorated rapidly from the start of 1997, especially internationally, with the financial and currency instability of various Southeast Asian countries, devaluation of the yen, and the slowdown in the Chinese economy. The won decreased in value to 1,000 to the dollar in November and continued to set new records, hitting an all-time low of 2,000 to the dollar.[2] This was compounded by tight foreign currency reserves created to depreciate the foreign debt that increased rapidly after 1995. In November, fluctuation in the Korean currency expanded from 2.25 percent in the past to 10 percent, and this accelerated the decline in the value of the won. The yen has continued to be weak relative to the dollar, but the won has lost value even more rapidly against the yen, and recently has been in excess of one yen to ten won.

South Korea joined the OECD at the end of 1996, but had to seek the financial support of the International Monetary Fund (IMF) and the United States. It is the second of the OECD member countries (after Mexico) that has needed IMF emergency assistance. The emergency aid from the IMF arrived at the beginning of December and the foreign currency shortfall has been relieved somewhat, but the future remains unclear. A total of several tens of billions of dollars is considered necessary to eliminate the foreign currency problem, and international financing for as much as $57 billion has been committed. The Korean economy, which has experienced growth over the long term, is currently faced with extremely difficult circumstances that affect its economic prowess, and at least the next two to three years will be required to rectify the situation.

Structural Problems and the Expansion Myth

The Need for Structural Reforms

Why did this economic slide occur? Why is the Korean economy faced with these difficulties? A review of the last decade or so suggests some answers.

The Korean economy has been through at least two periods of "structural adjustment" so far in the mid-1980s and the first half of the 1990s. Exports, which could be termed the lifeline of the Korean economy, increased rapidly in the latter half of the 1980s and mid-1990s. This increase coincided with a period when the yen was extremely strong against the dollar. Economic growth in the mid-1980s was due to the high yen after the Plaza Accord in the fall of 1985, and in 1995 the yen was pushed even higher. In both cases, Korea had been troubled by lack of growth in its export rate prior to the yen's increase in value, and commercial restructuring became an imperative. However, as noted, the high yen significantly revived the international competitiveness of Korean products in both the mid-1980s and mid-1990s. Due to this "good fortune," the Korean economy recovered prior to completion of its restructuring, and its commercial structure and organizations were never adequately revamped, leaving to this day a structure and organizations formed at the initial stages of its economic development. In terms of structure, South Korea has a pattern of industrialization known as "assembly-line industrialization" that is aimed at maximizing exports, and in terms of organization, the industrialization is centered on the conglomerates constituting this structure.

The assembly-line industrialization pattern is an attempt to ensure price competitiveness by importing natural resources (raw materials as well as parts), by installing a mass-production system supported by economies of scale (naturally, capital investments are significant), and by combining this with inexpensive labor.[3] Due to this structure, South Korea has consistently been in the red in its trade with Japan, from which it imports capital goods and components for assembly in Korea. The high yen strengthened the competitiveness of Korea's products in the international market, but this necessitated the importation of Japanese products that were proportionately higher priced. Thus, the high yen, although favorable for Korean exports, worked to increase the deficit with Japan. Trade with Japan aside, Korea's balance of trade with the rest of the world has been consistently in the red, except during the latter half of the 1980s.

The fundamental policies for resolving this trade imbalance include eliminating "assembly-line industrialization" and moving toward domestically producing the natural resources, raw materials, and parts. However, this is not easy because of the rapid pace of technological developments and the difficulty in amassing the requisite technological expertise. In addition, there is a limit to technological progress that South Korea can achieve on its own. Ultimately, capital investments are necessary and foreign currency is required for purchasing equipment.

After "privatization" began in 1987, Korea's debt level rose precipitously. From 1987 to the mid-1990s, the debt rose an average of 16 percent annually. During the same period, Taiwan's debt rose 11 percent and Japan's rose 3 percent, as announced by the Korean government. Further, inexpensive labor, an indispensable condition for "assembly-line industrialization," was lacking in the Korean economy.

In addition, the policy of industrialization centered on the *chaebol* was not reformed. The *chaebols* grew rapidly during the 1970s, a period of growth in the heavy and chemical industries. In 1973, the percentage of GNP represented by Korea's five largest *chaebol* was 3.5 percent, but this increased to 8.1 percent by 1978 and to 10 percent by 1983. The percentage began to decline thereafter, going down to as little as 6.2 percent by 1993, but increased again and reached 8.1 percent in 1995. This growth is the result of the government-sanctioned participation of the *chaebol* in the public sector under the slogan, "utilization of private sector vitality."[4] In other words, the administration of Kim Young Sam, which had achieved democratization and appeared to be aiming toward a market economy, was actually throwing more weight toward the chaebol.

A very interesting point here is that Taiwan, which also achieved "assembly-line industrialization" like Korea, has moved toward a favorable balance of trade. Taking just its trade with Japan, Taiwan has always been in the red, but it has achieved a profitable balance of trade with the rest of the world. Adequate research has not yet been done to explain the discrepancy, but a convincing explanation would be the difference in commercial organizations between Korea's focus on large corporations and Taiwan's fostering of medium and small corporations to form a flexible network.[5] The main characteristics of the Korean economy (its commercial structure and organizations) were extremely efficient at the initial stages of development, but as its economy increased in complexity, gradual adjustments should have been made. This is what I meant in speaking of "incomplete restructuring." A commercial structure with enormous assembly-line corporations and weak corporations that provide parts—that is, a commercial organization with enormous *chaebol* and weak small and medium-sized corporations—should have been reformed, but the reforms were postponed because restructuring Korea's international economy took precedence. What was advantageous in the short term brought about problems in the medium- to long-term.

If the problems stated above are seen from the perspective of technology, several points can be made. First, the pattern of assembly-line industrialization was, in one respect, also a pattern of industrialization by economizing on technology. The period in which Korea began to catch up with the industrialized countries was also a period of rapid technological innovation. Korea, which began industrializing while it still lacked sufficient technological experience, was forced to resort to equipment and machinery to produce products that would be acceptable to the world markets. Of course, Korea was able to enter the world markets because it made such rapid progress in improving the various types of machinery that it needed. To do this, Korea chose a direction that utilized technology that gave rise to new equipment and machinery, rather than technology based on accumulated human experience; that is to say, it chose a direction that gave it new technology by updating and perfecting machines. This brings to mind the assertion by Professor Klugman of MIT, who argued that the various countries that began to develop economically after Japan achieved its economic growth did so by increased capital investments and intensive commitment of labor, while lacking the accumulated technological experience of the advanced countries. In an economic observer's terms, this would probably be industrialization by "economizing on technology." The opposite of this kind of growth would be industrialization by "accumulation of technology," and Japan placed last among the developed countries with this pattern of economic growth. It was aided by a tradition that values craftsmen, one to which the accumulation of technology (technique) is fundamental. Around the time when Japan began to industrialize, technology was developing at a slower pace. And again, it had the societal foundations for accumulating technology and especially valued this as proper and good. Although the *zaibatsu* tended to form, numerous small and medium-sized corporations took shape around these.

Need to Support Industry

South Korea's balance of trade with the world has been consistently in the red, excluding the four years from 1986 to 1989. Its balance of trade with Japan has also been consistently in the red. The percentage of trade with Japan is relatively low, but from the perspective of balance of trade, one realizes that most of Korea's deficit arises from its trade with Japan. Therefore, Korea's economic problems can be understood by looking at the details of this trade.

Trade between Japan and Korea continues to be problematic for both countries, but rather than just remaining unresolved, the problems tend to grow. In 1996, both exports and imports decreased, but Korea's deficit did not shrink. Korea has continued to assert that the "Japanese market is closed," but although this assertion cannot be completely denied, a more fundamental explanation is the differences in the commercial structures and organizations of Japan and Korea. Regardless of the high yen, Korea was forced to import machinery, parts, and raw materials from Japan. And despite the high yen, the already firmly established Japanese industries, with their support industries for parts and raw materials, managed to ensure their competitive edge. They did so in part by switching to local production overseas and mainly by reducing costs as well as improving the quality of parts. Therefore, although imports of parts and raw materials from Korea expanded somewhat as a result of the high yen, the increase was not significant. It is the difference between the Japanese and Korean commercial structure and organizations that is manifest in the increasing deficit in Korea's trade with Japan.

For example, the majority of exports from Japan to Korea were of various kinds of machinery, and combined with other commercial equipment and components represent more than 80 percent of exports. Although not shown on the chart, durable consumer goods represent only a small portion. Looking at imports from Korea, machinery imports increased after the yen appreciated and represented one-third of all imports, but most were elements for semiconductors. These products are, needless to say, from large corporations and there was little machinery and few parts. For the sake of comparison, let us look at the imports to Korea for 1993. Various machinery made up 20.2 percent of all imports, and since elements for semiconductors made up 7.3 percent, various machinery increased by 13.1 percent, but semiconductors represented 11 percent of this. Products for small-medium and medium-sized corporations remained only a small percentage of imports. Rather, clothing, which is a representative product for small-medium and medium-sized corporations, declined from 17.3 percent to 10.7 percent. Even with the preceding simple analysis, it is clear that the Korean commercial structure is weak in terms of small and medium-sized corporations, as well as in its international competitiveness with products of these corporations. A look at Korean exports shows they are largely finished goods, cars, and electronic appliances, and even the raw materials and parts are mostly the type produced by a large corporation, like semiconductors or steel. In this regard, Taiwan has the opposite structure. Taiwanese exports of parts and raw materials are significant compared with those of Korea. On the other hand, the competitiveness of Japanese small-medium and medium-sized corporations is supported by the competitiveness of finished goods. Korea can thus reduce its imports from Japan by supporting industry and thereby improve its balance of trade.

However, in Korea there is a problem with demand and a limited labor force that restricts the extent to which the supporting industry can be fostered. In addition, the current situation has limited the number of small-medium corporations capable of producing quality goods. Since wages have risen to relatively high levels, high-end value-added goods must be produced, and the quality must be excellent. To do this, it is imperative to improve quality and productivity by introducing bold measures such as "localization."

The Expansion Myth

All developing countries tend to be prisoners of the expansion myth to some extent. It is assumed the higher the rate of growth, the greater the quantity of production; the more sales, the larger the market share and the investment. When these are combined with the government's economic policies, the ambitions of the individual corporations become a myth officially sanctioned by the country. Then the myth is actualized when the domestic market is still underdeveloped or when low-end entry in the world markets is possible.

However, ironically, the more the myth becomes a reality, the more the domestic market tends to reach limits, and the more difficult it becomes to participate even in the low end in international markets. To counterbalance the debt that has arisen, the country is forced to shift to higher value-added products, and barriers develop, such as lack of the requisite technology or technical skill and creativity. Cars serve as an example. Korean auto production grew rapidly in the first half of the 1980s with exports to North America. In addition, the favorable economy in the latter half of the 1980s greatly expanded domestic sales of cars. However, in the mid-1990s, domestic demand reached a plateau with sales of 1.6 to 1.7 million cars. Since domestic sales during the bubble economy in Japan were at about 6 million cars, this was comparable, considering the size of the Korean domestic market. In addition, exports were at a level of about 1 million cars. However, favorable economic conditions in the latter half of the 1980s through the first half of the 1990s accelerated investments to expand production, and under the current circumstances downward adjustments will probably be inevitable. But if the investment plans of all the companies are totaled, domestic production will reach 5 million cars by the year 2005. Furthermore, if plans for overseas production are added in, the figure becomes 10 million cars. Actualizing an expansion myth of this magnitude is not feasible.[6]

There is another Korean example of the expansion myth. Excessive investments in steel and special metals were a factor in the difficulties of several corporations. This economic sector was undeniably important to Korea. However, special metals, in particular, required the production of a wide variety of goods in small quantities, with strict demands for high quality. Consequently, whether Korea had the technology for this at the time became the issue. In summary, excessive investments were probably made in areas in which technological experience was lacking. This means that Korea must focus on helping individuals use technology more efficiently rather than pouring more capital into industry. This requires a shift from development by "economizing on technology" to development by "accumulation of technology," as mentioned earlier. Actually, the environment has been created for accumulation of the technology and technical skills for these supporting fields. Ironically, since "democratization" in 1987, the unemployment rate has declined and the difference in salaries between the large corporations and small-medium corporations has increased. The gap in salaries between large corporations of 500 employees or more and small-medium corporations of 29 employees or less has increased by close to 40 percent. This is due to the movement of employees between companies and will lead to an environment in which technology is accumulated outside the corporation or by the individual. Since the relationship between high growth and the supply of labor has traditionally been tight in Korea, and movement in the labor force has been at quite a high level, the technology utilized by corporations in production is fairly standardized, and most of this technology relies on equipment and machinery. The technology that the laborer in production holds should be standard and adequate. However, the technology required by the supporting industry, such as in machinery and parts, is specialized and unique rather than standard. This kind of technology requires the accumulation of a certain level of experience, and it is not favorable for the laborers to transfer between jobs frequently. Ironically, the current "conditionality" of the IMF will increase the unemployment rate, causing employees to remain at corporations, and potentially could foster in-house technology. It would be beneficial if this period were utilized to formulate technology and technical skills unique to each corporation.

Will industrial competitive strength increase? I have previously pointed out some issues concerning the economic growth of Korea in the 1980s. Was the growth real if the country was devaluing its currency during the growth? In addition, in a book published during the period at the end of the 1980s when the won continued to be high, I asserted that it would be a plus if adjustments were made to the commercial structure while the won gradually increased in value.[7] Needless to say, it would be beneficial for the balance of trade to be improved while the currency gained strength.

Let us look at the relationship between Japan's balance of trade and the exchange rate. Until 1970, the yen traded at a fixed rate of 360 to the dollar, but Japan switched to a fluctuating rate in 1971, and the trend was for the rate to increase. Therefore, except for the period around the Oil Shock, the balance of trade moved into the black beginning in the 1970s. In the 1980s, a positive balance was established and was criticized by companies worldwide, and the yen proceeded to gain in value. Entering the 1990s, the expanding trade imbalance finally slowed, but it is common knowledge that a significant imbalance remains. In the case of Korea, the trade balance was positive while the won continued to be high at the end of the 1980s, but the lower won continues and the trade deficit is expanding. On December 23, 1997, a record low was set of 2,000 won to the dollar. Since the beginning of 1998, the won has been at 1,700 to the dollar.

What method could be used to rectify this situation? There are the methods used by Korea in the past, such as devaluation of the won to improve price competitiveness temporarily. However, an OECD member country like Korea does not have the option of having its government authorities manipulate the country's currency in order to improve the balance of trade. Nor is this currently possible with the fluctuating markets since December of 1996.

A second method would be to reduce labor costs. Salary increases in 1996 were relatively low, but the results of this would be the same as those from the first method; that is, extending the supports for price competitiveness. The directions Korea can take in the future, as mentioned earlier, depend on whether or not competitiveness can be attained in areas other than prices.

The third method is to switch the way natural resources are distributed, from servicing a growth-driven ideology to supplying a mature economy. This means that even if the rate of economic growth declines slightly, the country must change its aim toward developing a replete economy, for example, by fostering support of industry and competitive small-medium corporations. To this end, the consciousness of the corporate man or woman and general citizen must be changed, not just that of the government authorities. If maximizing the growth rate and exports continue to be aims in the future, the methods used so far would not be bad. However, the trade deficit would not be reduced thereby and the commercial structure based on assembly-line and commercial organizations centered on large corporations would probably not be reformed. What is needed at this time is a commercial structure and organizations with an ideology based on research and development, and a switch to stable growth.

The Burden of Unification

The Korean economy is by no means small. It is eleventh in scale among the countries of the world. GNP in 1996 reached around $480 billion, and GNP per individual was over $10,500. In scale, this was nearly thirty times the GNP of the North and close to fifteen times the GNP per individual. Seen simply by cash flow, with a GNP for the North of $16 billion, the average GNP per individual for the North and the South combined in 1996 was about $7,300. This is large compared to the Southeast Asian countries if one excludes Singapore. This figure is equivalent to the GNP per individual of the South for 1992 and 1993, and if the South Korean people resolve to reduce living standards to the level of a few years ago, it would be possible to provide assistance to the North of about $140 billion annually. However, this is unlikely to happen. The reason is that companies are investing enough to maintain the living standards of the Korean people at above a $10,000 level, and even if the standard of living were lowered and they were able to economize, corporate investments and assets would go unused and make financial assistance to the North impractical.

Are there other possibilities for assisting the North? The consolidated tax obligation of the Korean people in 1996 was 81 trillion won, and the consolidated tax rate was 21 percent. If, for instance, this were raised to 30 percent, tax revenues would be 115 trillion won and 34 trillion could be appropriated to assist the North. This would be $34 billion at 1,000 won to the dollar, but the obligation per individual would be $755 (about 800,000 won). In other words, on average, this would be $2,500 (about 2.5 million won) per family. This plan would also be quite difficult to implement. Since a 1 percent consolidated tax rate would be the equivalent of about 4 trillion won, the maximum level by which the consolidated tax rate could be raised, considering the current economic conditions in Korea, would be about 2–3 percent. But by doing this, South Korea would be able to provide from 8 trillion to 12 trillion won for the North, or about $8 billion to $12 billion. In other words, the maximum sacrifice per individual would be about 180,000 to 270,000 won. This would be 600,000 to 900,000 won per family, and means that 4–5 percent of about 1.4 million won, an average monthly salary (1996), would be adequate for the cost of unification. This is not necessarily an impossibility. Furthermore, this figure is the equivalent of 40–60 percent of the actual GNP of the North for 1996 as estimated by South Korea.

The calculations made here indicate that the South Korean people could adequately support the North, if they earnestly wished to, with the economic capacity built over the past forty years, aside from recent economic difficulties. Of course, in order to apply these preliminary calculations, peace on the Korean Peninsula as well as a soft landing for the North are necessary conditions, and South Korea would have to overcome any economic difficulties to make the plan succeed. If turmoil were to result from the unification process, this would change the scenario completely. The following is a scenario premised on a peaceful resolution of the tension on the Korean Peninsula and on South Korea's having proceeded with the unification process.

Likely Scenario

Looking at just the rough figures given above, unification of the North and South would be almost impossible without a period of transition. In other words, the plan that is probably the most realistic would involve establishing this "transition period," providing about $8 billion to $12 billion in assistance to the North, and helping the North rebuild its economy with the cooperation of South Korea and other interested countries. Unless for some reason the demarcation line is eliminated, maintaining the line would be favorable. Even if Korea is not unified completely in all aspects, establishing a transition period would be an acceptable concept, since it would be generally acknowledged that unification had been achieved if communications, the free passage of individuals, and the circulation of money became a reality.

What role would South Korea play during this transition period? Basically, South Korea would need to play the role that Japan and the United States played in the initial phase of its own economic development. After the mid-1980s, Japan's portion of direct investments by other countries in Korea declined, but its role prior to that was significant. Technology transfer would be the same. The proportion of technology being transferred from Japan is tending to decline, but in the past it was significant.

Relying on estimates by the Bank of Korea, the GNP per individual for the North in 1996 was probably about $900. This may be a slight overestimation, but this is about equivalent to the GNP of South Korea in the mid-1970s. At that time, the population engaged in agriculture was just under 50 percent, and industry represented about 20 percent. Of course, wages were low and capital flowed from Japan and the United States to take advantage of this, resulting in the development of labor-intensive industries. In South Korea at that time, ensuring employment was the most important issue, and expanding this employment became the foundation for industrial development in Korea thereafter. Therefore, the first thing South Korea must do during a transition period is to build up industries in the North that are labor intensive, such as textiles, production of sundry goods, and simple electronic products. It would not matter if the industries were newly established or were transferred from South Korea, in which case, some measures could be taken to provide infrastructure for the transfer.

Corporate investments overseas will probably be reconsidered due to the current economic crisis in South Korea, but the Korean corporations may be able to reroute to the North a portion of investments that were to go to China or Vietnam. This will contribute to reforming the commercial structure in South Korea itself. A portion of overseas investment would be for the purpose of expanding abroad, and the small-medium corporations, troubled by declining revenues, would undoubtedly have fewer qualms about expanding into the North than into other parts of Asia. Even if the borders of the two countries are maintained, small-medium corporations could take advantage of the low wages of the North and even enjoy freedom from tariffs, as long as funds and goods were able to flow freely between North and South.

The entire industrial sector would become more efficient if employment was established in the North and the relatively less-efficient part of industry was moved to the South, providing profits for both parties. The South would move industries requiring a less-sophisticated labor force, and the impact would be felt when capital as well as labor was injected into, let us say, the parts of industry that require a sophisticated labor force. This would enable a smooth transition from an industrial development pattern ofeconomizing on technology to a pattern of accumulating technology.

However, caution must be exercised during this transition period. Basically, a business pace must be sustained. As indicated earlier, shifts of capital from South Korea to the North should be applied to the electrical, road, ports, and distribution systems. Learning from the experiences of South Korea, the North will probably incorporate the idea that the important commercial sectors should mostly be privately managed.

Simultaneous with development of industry, the rebuilding of agriculture is an important issue. The recent food shortages in the North were not entirely the fault of serious flooding. Rather, centrally controlled agriculture should be held to blame for the deterioration of soil quality because of overcultivation, poorly managed terraced fields that climb the mountainsides, deterioration in drainage of cultivated mountainsides, and consequent transformation of fertile land to salt fields. Therefore, ongoing public-works projects are necessary, such as soil revitalization and gradual reforestation of the mountains in South Korea. These projects will have to come from public funds. Moreover, food aid will probably be necessary each year during this period of rebuilding. This will also initially have to come from public funds.

Conclusion

South Korea itself is faced with an economic crisis. But regardless of whether overcoming this crisis is a top priority, the North is on the brink of economic collapse and South Korea is forced to assist the North, possibly carrying this to the point of unification. It will probably take from three to four years to reform the commercial structure of South Korea, and there is no proof that the complete collapse of the North will bring about a recovery of the South Korean economy. Even if the collapse of the North were to result in a recovery of the South Korean economy, it would still be difficult for Korea alone to support the North, and surrounding countries would bear some of the burden of supporting the North.

However, if a transition period were established during which South Korea could transfer its less-profitable industries and corporations to the North to take advantage of lower wages, not only would these industries be revitalized, but also industrialization would be promoted in the North. If industry in the South were simultaneously made more efficient, this could bolster economic recovery in the South, increase its resources to assist the North, and even reduce its requisite expenditures on behalf of the North. The problem is how to switch to this kind of positive circulation between the North and South and maintain the stable situation it requires. The role of the surrounding countries is to ensure that stability endures.

Notes

[1] Thereafter, this quasi-nationalization was voided due to issues raised by the IMF (Nihon Keizai Shimbun, December 27, 1997).

[2] At the beginning of 1998, regardless of announcements by the IMF and other international financial organizations as well as advance emergency assistance from the Japanese government, the won has remained weak—between 1,700 to 1,800 to the dollar.

[3] Concerning "assembly-line industrialization," refer to articles by Tamio Hattori (editor) in 1987 and 1988.

[4] Refer to Hattori, 1997.

[5] Refer to Hattori and Sato (editors), 1996.

[6] Various types of investments, including investments in the auto industry, are likely to be frozen or reconsidered due to the currently unstable currencies and economic turmoil.

[7] Refer to Hattori, 1988.

References

Hattori Tamio, "The Industrialization of Korea—a Diagram of Its Development," (1987).

Asia Research Institute, "The Development of Management in Korea," (1988).

Bunpodo, "Chaebol-Style Enterprise Development in Korea" *The Developing Economies*, Vol. XXXV, No. 4 (1997).

Hattori Tamio and Sato, "The Development Mechanisms of Korea and Taiwan," (1996); Asia Research Institute, Korea Statistics Bureau, "Major Indicators of the Korean Economy," (1997).

Seio Okomoto, "North Korea Handbook," Kodansha (1997).

Korea and Japan:

Engaged, but Distant

By Lee Sook-Jong,
Senior Fellow, Sejong Institute in Sungnam City, Korea

For most Koreans, Japan has been perceived as a "closely engaged but distant country." Closeness is felt in terms of geographic proximity and practical economic ties. As neighboring countries, Korea and Japan had been engaged in marine trade for five centuries (although there was more piracy by Japanese ships than trade along the southern coast of Korea). The Japanese invasion of Korea in the late sixteenth century did not change the passive engagement to an active one, mainly because both Yi-Dynasty Korea and Tokugawa Japan took an isolationist foreign policy stance, but also because Korea's medieval diplomacy extended official recognition only to China. Korean-Japanese economic exchange was limited to a few ports until fairly recently. In fact, active engagement between Korea and Japan was imposed suddenly with the Japanese encroachment on the Korean Peninsula in the late nineteenth century, which culminated in the Japanese annexation of Korea in 1910. Therefore, Korean-Japanese diplomatic history can trace its origins to barely one-hundred years ago, and the initial mode of active engagement was the problematic one of an oppressed-oppressor relationship.

The root of today's psychological distance between the two countries lies in this past history of Japanese occupation of Korea. The Koreans maintain a stronger sense of rivalry toward the Japanese than vice versa because their feeling of victimization by Japanese colonial rule has been intertwined with the zeal to catch up in terms of modernization. The powerful Korean sense of deprivation has not abated, and this presents a strong barrier to construction of mutual trust and understanding between the two nations. Because both countries prospered after the end of World War II, Korea and Japan have each developed and propagated their own myth of dominance and cultural superiority that stems from their ancient past. Psychological distance and rivalry, however, have been successfully contained within the framework of pragmatic cooperation between the two countries in at least two areas: economic and security.

Economic Cooperation

Korea and Japan are important economic partners. Korea is a major exporter of industrial goods to Japan and it relies on Japan for essential intermediate goods and high-technology products. Korea's exports to Japan amounted to US$17,049 million, while its imports stood at US$32,606 million in 1996. From another vantage point, Japan took in about 5 percent of its total imports from Korea in 1995, at the same time sending about 7 percent of its total exports to Korea. The Korean export market has been the second-largest for Japan in the 1990s, only surpassed by exports to the United States.

While the mutual contribution to economic dynamism is significant, the Korea-Japan trade relationship reflects their economic status gap, i.e., between Japan as an economic superpower and Korea as a newly industrialized country. Korea's trade deficit with Japan has been growing, due in large measure to the rapidly rising demand for Japanese intermediary goods and technology with the increasing sophistication of Korea's industrial structure and its expanding capital investment. Korea's trade deficit with Japan rose from US$7,859 million in 1992 to US$15,557 million in 1995. Japan's trade surplus with Korea accounted for 13.1 percent of Japan's total surplus in 1995. The growing trade deficit with Japan has contributed to the popular notion that Japan gets more from Korean-Japanese trade than vice versa. Nevertheless, the majority of Koreans regard Japan as the most important country for the development of the Korean economy, and the idea that economic cooperation with Japan is crucial for Korea's future is widely shared among Koreans.

Mutual Security Cooperation

Less publicly recognized is Korea's security ties with Japan. Korea and Japan have been allies through the United States, with which each of these countries has a bilateral military alliance. The Korean government has faithfully pursued security cooperation with Japan within this Korea–U.S.–Japan triple alliance framework. Despite the official line of Korea–Japan security cooperation, the popular perceptions of Koreans lag far behind in terms of support for the government's cooperation with Japan. For many Japanese, it would be quite surprising to learn that a majority of Koreans consider Japan a major threat to their national security. Viewing an official ally as an enemy state is not simply a distorted Korean reaction based on the confusing psychological distrust with real security issues. Rather, much of the problem lies in the facts that first, the security cooperation between Korea and Japan is an unclear one, with no official written rules or treaty, and second, that this cooperation is rather indirect and feeble, cemented only by the encouragement and support of their common ally—the United States. To the extent that Korea-Japan security ties are subject to the conditions of the Korea–U.S.–Japan triple alliance, it is likely to change when the U.S. commitment to this framework is weakened.

Clearly, Korea and Japan share the same interest in securing peace and stability in Northeast Asia, and leaders of both countries share the need to build a constructive forward-looking partnership in both security and economic affairs. The challenge facing the two governments in this regard is twofold. One need is to pursue policies for reconciliation, which can contribute to construction of a trustworthy relationship at the mass level. The second is to set concrete agendas to expand security cooperation between the two countries. At the moment, the second task appears to be feasible only after realization of the first one. Without true reconciliation that frees Korea and Japan from the colonial past and establishes mutual trust, Korean-Japanese cooperation will remain superficial.

This paper examines Korea's public perceptions toward Japan and Korea-Japan relations. The study is motivated by the belief that foreign-policy makers should take into serious consideration the perceptions of ordinary citizens. Korea's Japan policy is particularly sensitive to public opinion in Korea. Without popular support, Korea's nascent democratic government would have great difficulty undertaking potentially controversial actions in times of emergencies. Needless to say, official foreign policies become inconsistent and ineffective when they are at complete odds with prevailing public opinion. The goal of this paper is to show the dual nature of the Korean attitude toward Korean-Japanese affairs, i.e., the pragmatic cooperation that stands in contrast to the feelings of distance, disapproval, and mistrust. The data set is from the 1996 RAND–*Joong Ang Daily* newspaper survey (hereafter referred to as the RAND survey). The survey was conducted September 16–30, 1996, with a sample of 1,050 adults aged twenty and over from throughout Korea except for Cheju Island. The survey was based on interviews, using a structured questionnaire (which the author helped develop). The sample error was ± 3.1 percent with a 95 percent confidence level.

Korean Public Perceptions of Japan

In the mind of the average Korean, the image of the Japanese and Japan can best be described as dual. On the one hand, the image is highly positive, based on Japan's economic performance and social stability. On the other hand, Koreans harbor a negative image, focused on Japanese motivation both at the individual and national levels. Since the RAND survey data does not include the image questions, longitudinal data from surveys conducted by Korea's *Dong-A Daily* and Japan's *Asahi Shimbun* over the past fifteen years was used. As seen in Table 1, the most popular positive images Koreans have about the Japanese are "diligent," "unified," and "good mannered," while popular negative images are "egoistic," "calculating," and "not trustworthy."

Table 1. Korea's Images of the Japanese People (N = 2,000; %)

	1984	1988	1990	1995	1996
diligent	14.2	13.5	12.8	19.4	20.1
unified	23.9	27.8	29.8	25.7	18.7
egoistic	18.6	18.4	20.1	20.9	24.9
calculating	13.8	14.4	15.6	13.0	15.5
not trustworthy	11.0	9.7	8.2	7.2	6.1
good mannered	7.2	5.0	7.2	6.6	8.5
oppressive	3.1	1.4	2.2	3.3	--
emotional	--	--	--	--	3.1
able	3.3	3.4	2.8	2.6	2.2
others	4.9	6.5	1.4	1.3	0.9
TOTAL	**100.0**	**100.0**	**100.0**	**100.0**	**100.0**

Note: The 1996 survey replaced "oppressive" with "emotional."

Korea's image of Japan as a nation is centered on two elements: Japan's current economic status and its past history with Korea. The Koreans view the Japanese economy at two levels, one focused on Japan's national economy per se and the other on the impact of the Japanese economy on other countries. As Table 2 demonstrates, the image of Japan is represented by economic power and high technology, but at the same time, Japan is perceived as having invaded the economies of other countries and being passive in its economic cooperation with Korea. Since this national image question is structured with suggested items, the free association question was checked to get a fairer picture of the Korean answers. In the 1995 survey of *Dong-A Daily,* Koreans were asked to write down what is freely associated with the word *Japan.* In this open-ended question, the associated images of Japan were, in order of frequency, "Japanese things" (19.6 percent), "calculating one's own interest" (14.3 percent), "kindness" (14.0 percent), "animosity/anti-Japanese feelings" (13.9 percent), "economic development" (11.1 percent), "war" (9.3 percent), "colonial rule/historical "sufferings" (6.4 percent), "neighboring country" (3.0 percent), and "advanced nation" (2.6 percent). One noticeable recent trend is the substantial increase in the number of Koreans who believe that Japan has become less willing to acknowledge its past colonial oppression and to pay compensation for it. This reflects the growing anti-Japanese feelings associated with the Tokdo (Takeshima Island) controversy that emerged from the negotiations over the Exclusive Economic Zone between Korea and Japan.

Table 2: Images of Japan as a nation (N = 2,000; %)

	1984	1988	1990	1995	1996
less willing to accept or compensate colonial	9.6	11.2	13.4	15.9	31.7
oppression	31.0	23.8	30.9	30.6	23.5
economic power	21.6	16.5	20.6	24.6	17.5
invading other country's economy	7.3	9.1	5.9	4.9	6.3
passive for economic cooperation with Korea	--	--	--	--	6.3
oriented to being a military power	6.9	6.7	0.9	0.6	0.9
lacking in watching North Korea	2.3	2.8	1.7	1.3	--
politics is stable	2.1	2.3	0.8	0.6	0.9
freedom of speech	--	--	2.8	2.2	1.9
cherishing tradition	--	--	--	--	0.1
cultural imperialism	2.7	7.3	2.1	1.2	0.7
others					
TOTAL	**100.0**	**100.0**	**100.0**	**100.0**	**100.0**

Note: 1996 survey replaced "politics is stable" with "oriented to being a military power."

Role Model

Although Korean images of Japan and the Japanese are dualistic, in almost every survey of the "big four" surrounding Korea, Japan is picked as the role model for Korea, ahead of the United States, China, and Russia. But when the Koreans are asked to choose the best role model with other national options or with specific aspects of national performance, Japan's status as the best role model tends to be limited to economic realms. In the RAND survey asking the role model for specific items, Japan does not get high Korean approval (see Table 3). To the question, "Among Japan, China, Germany, the United States, which country is the best role model for Korea? Write in if it is another country," answers were skewed to the listed countries. Among the four countries compared, Japan was regarded as the best role model for maintaining social order and managing business enterprises, and as the second best for science-technology and environmental protection. For the remaining eight elements, however, Japan was ranked third, only ahead of China. Thus, apart from the economic and social category, Japan was not regarded favorably by the Koreans.

Table 3. Best Role Model for Korea (N = 1,050; %)

	Japan	China	Germany	United States
Business firms	42.9 (1)	4.4	13.9	26.2
Science-Technology	31.8 (2)	3.4	24.4	36.0
Maintaining social order	29.5 (1)	8.0	26.3	16.5
Protecting the environment	21.7 (2)	4.8	36.4	20.7
Lifestyle	20.3 (3)	8.5	28.8	24.1
Education	19.0 (3)	4.2	34.1	29.6
Ethics	13.9 (3)	10.1	23.8	15.2
Government	13.2 (3)	5.3	20.0	41.6
Social justice	13.2(3)	6.2	32.9	27.6
Role of women	12.9 (3)	5.9	17.8	43.6
Cultural achievement	12.1 (3)	9.1	28.3	27.7
Individual opportunity	9.7 (3)	4.5	16.0	58.4

Emotional Ties

Geographic proximity of nation-states can foster competition and mutual distrust rather than cooperation and trust, especially when they are, or are perceived to be, equal powers. The United Kingdom and France prior to this century cannot be regarded as friendly neighbors, and their cultural rivalry remains to this day. Since its consolidation into a strong modern state, Germany has been watched closely by its neighboring countries, especially by France.

In this section, Korea's emotional ties with Japan and the Japanese are examined by posing two questions. One is a thermometer question, and the other is Korea's self-assessment concerning how other countries might view Koreans.

In the thermometer question, which asked the respondents to rank their feelings toward seventeen countries on a scale of 0 to 100, Japan was ranked second from last, above only North Korea (see Table 4). Japan was in the 40-point range, which puts it in the same group with Iran and Libya. This lack of warm feelings toward Japan is in stark contrast to the close security and economic ties Korea has with Japan.

The response is a strong example of the fact that close economic and security ties and the acceptance of Japan as the best role model do not necessarily translate into positive feelings. It also bodes ill for building a trusting, long-term relationship and for expanding security ties with Japan. The mistrust and psychological deprivation the Koreans feel toward Japan is further illustrated by the next question.

Table 4. Average Thermometer Point for 17 Selected Countries (100 = positive, 0 = not positive)

High (around 60 point)	Medium (around 50 point)	Low (around 40 point and below)
United Kingdom (60.4)	Israel (53.1)	Iran (42.7)
Germany (60.0)	Taiwan (52.4)	Libya (41.8)
France (59.8)	China (51.2)	Japan (41.7)
Singapore (59.3)	Brazil (50.1)	North Korea (27.0)
United States (58.5)	Saudi Arabia (49.2)	
	Thailand (48.1)	
	Indonesia (47.5)	
	Russia (47.0)	

To the question, "Do you think most Japanese (or Americans or Chinese) respect Koreans or do they look down on Koreans?" a great majority of Koreans responded that the Japanese look down on them. Specifically, 89.7 percent of the Koreans think the Japanese look down on the Koreans, while 73.3 percent believe the Americans do so in varying degrees. In contrast, 63.5 percent of the Koreans believe the Chinese respect the Koreans (see Table 5). It is understandable that Koreans feel ignored by those living in a richer country such as Japan or the United States, while they feel respected by the Chinese, whom they obviously consider poorer. It is interesting to note, however, that the Koreans think the Japanese look down on them more than the Americans do, even though the Korean respondents must know that the United States exercises greater influence on Korean affairs. This reflects the sense of humiliation that the Koreans still feel over having once been occupied by the Japanese.

Table 5. Foreigners' Attitudes toward Koreans (N = 1,050; %)

Japanese Attitudes toward Koreans				
Respect		Look down		Don't know
3.6		89.7		6.7
American Attitudes toward Koreans				
Strongly respect	Somewhat respect	Somewhat look down	Strongly look down.	Don't know
1.6	18.9	64.2	9.1	6.3
Chinese attitudes toward Koreans				
Strongly respect	Somewhat respect	Somewhat look Down	Strongly look down.	Don't know
--	58.1	20.7	1.2	14.6

Note: For reasons unknown, the question on Japanese attitudes was asked with three categories of "respect," "look down," and "don't know," which differ from the questions regarding American and Chinese attitudes.

Power, Role, and Vital Interest Perceptions

This part examines how Koreans perceive Japanese power and Japan's importance to the national interest of Korea.

Power Perceptions

When asked the open-ended question, "What country do you think will be the greatest economic power of the next century?" more Koreans picked Japan (35.6 percent) than China (25.8 percent) or the United States (21.8 percent) (see Table 6). However, more Koreans believe the United States (42.5 percent) will be a greater military power in the next century than Japan (23.6 percent) or China (20.5 percent). Many Koreans share the idea that Japanese military power in the twenty-first century will continue to be limited in relation to Japan's economic power.

Table 6. Perception of Japanese Power in the Twenty-First Century

	Japan	United States	China
No. 1 Economic Power	35.6%	21.8%	25.8%
No. 1 Military Power	23.6%	42.5%	20.5%

International Role Perceptions

A great majority of the Koreans also think Japan will play a greater role in the world ten years from now than it does today (see Table 7). Although the expectations regarding Japanese role expansion are not high compared with those for China or Korea, a majority of Koreans expect Japan's international role will be expanded in the near future, whereas only slightly more Koreans expect the international role of the United States to remain the same.

Table 7: International Role Expansion Perception

	Greater Role	Same as Today	Lesser Role	Don't Know
China	1.0	1.8	1.0	1.8
Korea	8.0	20.0	6.0	2.0
Japan	74.8	39.9	1.3	2.0
United States	47.6	44.7	10.5	1.7
Germany	1.0	57.0	11.9	7.6
Indonesia	8.0	49.8	7.4	13.4

Though recognizing an expanding Japanese role in the future, the Koreans are wary of such expansion in the military area. To the question, "If the Japanese international role expands to a military role, how would it affect Korea?" 64.7 percent of Koreans stated that military role expansion would be bad for Korea. Only 17.9 percent said it would be good for Korea, while 7.1 percent said it would make no difference. In the same vein, opposition to permanent Japanese membership in the UN Security Council exceeded support by 10 percent (see Table 8; a four-scale measure where "strongly oppose" equals 1 point and "strongly support" 4 points, the average score was 2.34).

Table 8. Japanese Permanent Membership in the UN Security Council (N = 1,050; %)

Strongly support	Somewhat support	Somewhat oppose	Strongly oppose	Don't know
4.9	33.3	34.1	14.0	13.7

Vital Interest

The Koreans think the so-called surrounding big four powers are more important for Korea's national interest than any other country or region (see Table 9). Each of the four powers, however, is viewed differently in terms of its degree of importance for Korea's national interest. The position of the United States as the most important country for Korea's national interest is beyond challenge, and Russian saliency usually comes last among the big four powers. Japan or China is generally viewed as the second most important for Korea's vital interest. This pattern is consistent in many surveys. In the RAND survey, Japan ranked as the second most important country for Korea; 57.5 percent of Koreans think Korea has a vital interest in Japan, and 34.7 percent of Koreans think Korea has a large but not vital interest in Japan.

Table 9. Countries in Which Korea Has a Vital Interest (N = 1,050; %)

	Has a vital interest	Large but not vital interest	Not much interest at all	Don't know
United States	76.0	19.5	3.2	1.4
North Korea	61.1	17.1	18.3	3.4
Japan	57.5	34.7	6.6	1.2
China	52.7	37.3	8.0	2.0
Russia	25.4	46.0	22.0	6.5
Germany	19.6	53.2	21.3	5.9
Taiwan	17.1	53.3	24.2	5.4
Saudi Arabia	13.8	48.2	31.5	6.5
Brazil	8.5	39.4	43.1	8.9
Indonesia	8.2	40.9	42.4	8.5
Vietnam	7.1	37.5	44.2	11.2
South Africa	6.6	26.0	55.5	11.9
Israel	6.5	32.0	50.3	11.2
Iran	6.0	39.4	45.2	9.5
India	5.5	34.8	48.8	10.9
Poland	4.5	24.9	56.4	14.2

Rivalry and Threat Perceptions

As we have seen in an earlier section, the Koreans have yet to develop amicable emotional ties with the Japanese instead of maintaining their dislike or mistrust of Japan. Given a contradictory combination of active engagement and lack of trust, the Koreans harbor a sense of rivalry and consider Japan a threat to their well-being. On the question of assessing each of twelve threats to Korea's vital interest over the next ten years, the competition with Japan in foreign export markets and military buildup scored number one and two respectively. "Trade war with Japan" scored 3.49 ("no threat"=1, "less important threat"=2, "somewhat important threat"=3, "very critical threat"=4), and "The development of Japan as a major military power" scored 3.44. And to the question of "In thinking about the future, is Japanese investment in East Asia positive or negative for Korea?" 64.8 percent of Koreans answered "negative" while 26.5 percent said "positive."

However, the Koreans fear future economic competition from China more than from Japan (see Table 10). Many Koreans think that fast-growing China will catch up with Korea in the near future, while Korea remains behind Japan, which is too far advanced in terms of technology and investment capabilities. On the other hand, Koreans feel any military rivalry and security threat will come more from Japan than from China. As shown in Tables 11 and 12, almost half of the Korean respondents think Japan will be Korea's chief military rival after unification, and more than half point to Japan when asked, "Which of the following countries represents the greatest future danger to Korea's military security?"

Table 10. Korea's Biggest Economic Competitor in the Next 10 Years (N = 1,050; %)

China	Japan	Taiwan	United States	Thailand/Other S.E. Asian Companies	Other/DK
46.1%	29.1%	7.8%	6.5%	5.4%	5.0%

Table 11. Korea's Chief Military Rival After Unification (N = 1,050; %)

Japan	China	United States	Russia	No One	Other
47.6	31.5	13.8	5.3	1.5	0.3

Table 12. Greatest Danger to Korean Security (N = 1,050; %)

China	Japan	Russia	United States	Other/No Answer
32.9	54.0	5.0	5.9	2.3

A "no nuke policy" is not popular among Koreans, who usually consider self-defense capability essential for national security. In response to the statement, "Korea should never have nuclear weapons," 42.9 percent disagreed "strongly" and 36.0 percent "somewhat," while only 5.6 percent agreed "strongly," and 12.1 percent "somewhat" (see Table 13). When the respondents were offered three scenarios, the need for defensive nuclear armament of Korea was most strongly felt in the event of Japanese nuclear armament. A great majority of the respondents believed Korea must acquire nuclear weapons if Japan or North Korea do so, or if the Korea–U.S. alliance were to end. The average score indicating support for Korea's nuclear armament is higher in the case of Japanese acquisition of nuclear weapons (3.53, from "strongly disagree"=1 to "strongly agree"=4) than in the case of North Korea's acquisition (3.49) or the end of the ROK–U.S. alliance (3.42). This again is a strong indication of Koreans' perception of Japan as a major threat to their national security.

Table 13. Nuclear Armament of Korea (N = 1,050; %)

	Korea should acquire nuclear weapons				
	Strongly Disagree	Somewhat Disagree	Somewhat Agree	Strongly Agree	Don't Know
if Japan does	1.4	4.6	33.4	59.1	1.5
if North Korea does	1.8	6.4	32.4	58.8	0.7
if the ROK–U.S. alliance is ended	2.1	7.7	34.4	53.1	2.7

The Koreans highly value the close bilateral ties with the United States, Japan, and China in their foreign policy goals, since these three nations are perceived to be critical to Korea's national interest. But there is stronger feeling about the need to build closer ties with China and the United States than with Japan. "Building closer ties with Japan" scored 3.09, while "building closer ties with China" and "strengthening the ROK–US alliance" scored 3.29 and 3.16 respectively ("very important"=4 points, "somewhat important"=3 points, "somewhat less important"=2 points, "not important"=1 point).

The next section examines how the Koreans view Korean-Japan bilateral ties in terms of specific issues and how they see the power balance and security alignment among Japan, the United States, and China.

Korea-Japan Economic Relations

It is widely known that Korea's industrial policy of the past several decades has been aimed at strengthening its own national capital base, which contributed to the relatively low level of direct foreign capital investment. The national industrial policy echoes the lukewarm Korean attitude toward courting Japanese capital. The Koreans have been far less welcoming toward Japanese capital than the Southeast Asians. To the question of "Would you like to see more, less, or about the same Japanese investment in Korea?" the answers are divided almost equally between "less" (31.6 percent), "more" (27.5 percent), and "about the same" (32.2 percent). As for the desired amount of trade, the pattern of the answers is similar, although more Koreans chose "more trade" over status quo and "less trade." Specifically, 36.9 percent chose "more trade," 34.9 percent "about the same," and 23.2 percent "less."

However, the Koreans consider Japan as their most important economic partner. To the question "Which country would you say is Korea's most important economic partner?" half of the respondents chose Japan over China (23.7 percent) and the United States (11.9 percent). And the majority (67.5 percent) of the respondents believes that Japan makes products of higher quality than the United States (9.5 percent) or Germany (14.1 percent).

When one considers such highly positive views of Japan's economic performance and the recognition of Japan as Korea's most important economic partner, Korea-Japan economic ties will likely continue to be close and solid, even though the Koreans see the trade deficit with Japan as being unfair and the rising Japanese investment in East Asia as a negative force on Korea. Feelings of economic competition and rivalry on the part of the Koreans, however, are likely to have positive effects on Korea-Japan economic ties and cooperation.

Korea-Japan Security Relations

In order to tap Korean attitudes regarding security cooperation with Japan, several hypothetical questions were asked. To the question "If North Korea invades South Korea, should Korea accept support from Japan?" 57.2 percent said "accept" while 34.7 percent said "don't accept" (see Table 14). When those who agreed to accept Japanese support were asked to choose the type of support, the absolute majority preferred noncombatant support, such as financial assistance, to the dispatch of Japanese armed forces.

Table 14. Security Cooperation with Japan if Invaded from North Korea

If invaded from North Korea should South Korea accept support from Japan? (N = 1,050; %)		
Accept	Don't Accept	Don't Know
57.2	34.7	8.1

If North Korea invades South Korea what type of support should Korea accept from Japan? (N = 601; %)			
Financial Assistance	Noncombatant Support	Japanese Self-Defense Forces	Don't Know
37.3	39.1	17.5	6.1

Regional Security Alignments

Many Koreans see the regional balance of power as crucial for their survival. With the perceived decline in U.S. commitment to securing peace and stability in the Northeast Asian region, the rise of China and Japan, and instability in Russia, the Koreans are concerned that Korea's national security will be vulnerable to the conflicts and the hegemonic power competition in the region. According to the RAND survey data, the Koreans support the idea of developing closer political and military ties with China or Japan if one of them becomes a threat to Korea (see Table 15). A Japanese threat appeared to consolidate a Korea-China alignment somewhat more than a Chinese threat consolidated a Korea-Japan security alignment. To the question "Would you support or oppose developing closer political and military ties with Japan in the event that China threatens Korea's security?" 60.7 percent of Koreans supported the idea. On the other hand, to the question "If Japan threatens Korea's security, would you support or oppose closer Korean political and military ties with China?" 81.7 percent supported the idea.

Table 15. Security Alignment If Threats Exist from China or Japan

Strongly Support	Somewhat Support	Somewhat Oppose	Strongly Oppose	Don't Know
If threat from China, should Korea have closer ties with Japan?				
13.3	47.4	23.3	5.6	10.3
If Japan threatens Korea, should Korea use China as a balance?				
25.4	56.3	11.1	1.5	5.6

The Koreans also think the ROK–U.S. alliance is important not only for providing regional security and ensuring against a crisis on the Korean Peninsula, but also for balancing regional power relations. Table 16 shows the Koreans think a ROK–U.S. alliance can contain Japan, Russia, and China. It is interesting to note that the Koreans believe a security alliance with the United States can contain Japan more successfully than China, although the difference is not large.

Table 16. Roles of ROK–US Alliance (N = 1,050; %)

ROK–US Alliance	(Avery Score)	Strongly Disagree	Somewhat Disagree	Somewhat Agree	Strongly Agree	Don't Know
Provides stability in East Asia	(3.14)	1.4	11.0	54.9	27.2	5.6
Ensures against crisis on Korean Peninsula	(3.05)	3.3	13.6	49.2	25.0	8.9
Prevents Japan from becoming a military power	(2.96)	4.8	18.8	45.7	24.9	5.8
Ensures against revival of Russian threat	(2.71)	5.5	28.8	41.8	14.0	9.8
Contains China	(2.60)	6.2	36.0	38.5	11.2	8.1

Summary and Policy Suggestions

The Korean mass perceptions regarding Japan can be summarized as follows:

1. Japan is the biggest economic power most important to Korea's vital interest. Many Koreans have a high regard for Japan's current economic performance and view Japan as the number one economic power in the twenty-first century. On the other hand, the Koreans view the rise of Japanese military power as being limited, while believing the United States will maintain its military superpower position. The Koreans also think that the expansion of the Japanese international role in the future will be far smaller than that of China and their own country. Overall, the Koreans consider Japan to be a country in which Korea has a vital interest, whose significance for Korea is second only to that of the United States.
2. Distant emotional ties and mistrust of Japan affect Korean perceptions of Japan. Overall, the Koreans do not have positive feelings toward the Japanese. Japan belongs to the group of nations they

like the least, and they feel that the Japanese look down on Koreans. Korean mistrust of Japan is highlighted in their viewing of Japan as the greatest danger to their security. Koreans believe that Japan's emergence as a major military power will be a grave threat to Korea's interest in the next ten years, and they support the nuclear armament of Korea if Japan acquires nuclear weapons.

3. Korea-Japan relations have a two-track diplomacy. The positive evaluation of Japanese economic performance would encourage pragmatic developments in economic cooperation with Japan, although the Koreans do question the motivation and fairness of Japanese economic activities. Koreans regard Japan as their most important economic partner. However, they are not ready for military cooperation with Japan even if North Korea invades. The Koreans tend to think the ROK–U.S. alliance can prevent Japan from becoming a military power, and they want to balance the Japanese threat by developing closer ties with China. They seem to have a two-track mind in diplomacy toward Japan. One is active economic engagement and pragmatist cooperation on the one hand, and limited security engagement, complicated by a sense of distrust and disapproval, on the other.

Based on the preceding summary, one can make several policy suggestions for closer Korea-Japan relations. The Korea-Japan economic relationship is likely to remain solid and to expand in the near future. Although the Koreans harbor a sense of suspicion and economic rivalry toward Japan, this need not dampen closer economic cooperation. On the contrary, the drive to catch up would contribute to the growth and dynamism of the two economies.

The problems in Korea-Japan relations in the future seem to lie mainly in security cooperation. Much has been said about the necessity to build closer security ties between Korea and Japan because the current framework of the Korea–U.S.–Japan triple alliance is expected to be modified. The Koreans feel particularly vulnerable to the changing power balance of the United States, China, and Japan and its ramifications for regional stability. So far, Korea has pursued an active engagement policy vis-à-vis China and Russia mainly by developing economic ties and status quo policies in maintaining close security ties with the United States and Japan. Any progress in building more direct and closer security ties with Japan is linked to the conditions of this double-edged strategy.

Although Korea's security alignment can change with various scenarios, one can say that, depending on the Korean mass perception, direct security linkage with Japan appears to be unlikely. Unless Koreans build a sense of trust and understanding regarding what Japan pursues, it will remain difficult for Korea to construct closer bilateral security ties with Japan. One can argue that public opinion is not crucial to the development of security relations. But Korean mass perceptions of Japan do matter because Korea's relationship with Japan has been the most sensitive foreign relationship, and it is therefore easily politicized.

The Korean government, which has sometimes used anti-Japanese feelings for domestic political purpose, would find it difficult to persuade people to accept a greater Japanese role. But it is ultimately Japan that has to win the hearts of the Korean people, if it truly wishes to be accepted as a neighbor, by settling the controversies over past history. And policy planners should keep in mind that changing people's hearts at a time when foreign policy changes are needed would take much more time than changing the foreign policies.

Mutual Understanding and Confidence-Building in the Internet Era

By Murooka Tetsuo,
Associate Professor at the National Institute of Defense Studies in Tokyo*

Friendly relations between Japan and the Republic of Korea (hereafter Korea) is one of the indispensable factors for peace and prosperity in the Asia-Pacific. Though the two countries have enjoyed close relations in economic, academic, and other various fields, distrust between Japanese and Koreans still remains. This psychological environment is hampering further progress of the bilateral relationship. However, these traditional and stagnant settings have seemingly been challenged by the Information Revolution since the early 1990s. The author would like to examine whether such new trends will promote the mutual understanding between the two nations.

In both Japan and Korea, the number of personal computers (PCs) has rapidly increased since the early 1990s. Many of them are connected to online services. The number of subscribers to such services reached 4.8 million in Japan and surpassed 2 million in Korea in 1996 as the Internet has rapidly gained popularity in Korea and Japan in the mid-1990s. Japan had 900,000 host computers for the Internet and Korea

** The opinions expressed here do not necessarily reflect those of the National Institute of Defense Studies, The Japan Defense Agency or the Japanese Government.*

130,000 as of July 1997. The number of Internet users is estimated as 5 million in Japan and 1.55 million in Korea.

In the early period of the Information Revolution, Korean PC experts made efforts to handle Japanese on the operating systems (OSs) and communication applications of their computers. Their Japanese counterparts also tried to use Korean. By so doing, they devised various techniques to access each other through the net with Japanese and Korean. It was noteworthy that they did so even before Apple, Netscape, and Microsoft developed and sold multilingual systems and applications. With such products, we can handle two-byte languages such as Korean more easily than before.

The Internet has contributed in mutual trust between Japanese and Koreans since its advent. Its decreased cost of communication allows the Japanese and Koreans to be able to "talk" with their "pen pals" in the other country to collect information about their neighboring nation more effectively. The Net, however, also brings about negative factors to Japanese-Korean mutual understanding. For example, some people express extreme opinions or groundless rumors against Koreans or Japanese on the Net. This type of discussion often develops into a vicious circle of abuses.

As we have seen, the Internet provides opportunities and possibilities to facilitate mutual understanding between Japan and Korea. Both countries, especially the governments, should provide information through the Net in the counterpart's language. They also should strengthen infrastructures as language education (especially Korean language education in Japan) and cultural exchanges between Japan and Korea.

Unification and the Social and Cultural Heterogeneity of North and South

By Kohari Susumu,
Shizuoka Prefecture University

Introduction

The Korean Peninsula, as a whole, is a region inhabited by people with the same ethnic background.[1] The common social and cultural history of this single ethnic group goes far back in history, and a homogeneous ethnic culture has been maintained. The originally warring Koguryo, Paekche, and Silla kingdoms that were to become the Three Kingdoms (A.D. 313 to 676), were autonomous societies under separate, independent rulers, but fundamentally they shared a common cultural tradition.[2] Even under the Japanese colonial occupation (1910–1945), the Koreans were integrated socially and culturally.

After the war, the Korean Peninsula was divided into North and South and, since 1948, has existed as two separate countries, the Republic of Korea (South Korea) and the Democratic People's Republic of Korea (North Korea). Although the country is divided, the people are ethnically the same, speak the same language, and share the same cultural traditions. However, the societies and cultures of the two countries, North Korea and South Korea, are no longer completely homogeneous. Due to differences in their political systems, economic systems, and foreign relations, the social and cultural heterogeneity of North and South has become conspicuous.

Because of reports of systemic instability in North Korea, such as the severely depressed economy, which has caused food shortages and an increasing flow of refugees, discussion of Korean unification is beginning to sound realistic. One theory is that North and South Korea may be able to attain unification suddenly due to a "collapse" of North Korea.

The confusion likely to arise if these systems that have diverged for close to fifty years are unified, can be seen in the process of German unification. Of course, German political and economic consolidation has been difficult, but some social and cultural aspects of unification have also caused problems.[3] If unification of the Korean Peninsula is achieved, it will probably be the same. South Korea is assessing the unification process; that is, calculating the requisite "unification costs" of bringing the two countries together.[4] Observers have cited the social and cultural disruption caused by refugees from North Korea who are attempting to live in South Korean society—problems caused by the basic homogeneity of South Korea.

After first investigating the extent to which heterogeneity has developed between North and South Korea since division of the country, this paper will point out the social and cultural problems likely to arise from unification. Finally, it will discuss issues that South Korea and the surrounding countries will have to face after unification in order to resolve these problems.

Social and Cultural Heterogeneity in North and South Korea

North and South Korea have historically shown distinct regional characteristics. During the Three Kingdom period, the southern region consisted of the separate Silla and Paekche societies and the northern region consisted of Koguryo. In contrast to the south, where the grain belt is vast and the climate relatively mild, the north is very mountainous and winters are severe. Due to these geographic differences, differences in customs have existed through history. Even during the Japanese colonial occupation, a distinction was made between South Korea and North Korea (at the time, both called by abbreviated contemptuous labels), with the unique regional characteristics and characteristics of the inhabitants cited officially.[5] Those born in the northern region of the Korean

Peninsula were depicted as being strong in survival skills, and those born in the south as being reserved and even-tempered.[6]

However, governments with contrary ideologies and social systems were established in the North and South in 1948. The social and cultural heterogeneity that has arisen since division of the Korean Peninsula can be investigated by focusing mainly on the unique characteristics of North Korea.

First, if the societies of North and South were broadly defined, South Korea would be a society characterized by individualism and North Korea would be a socialist society characterized by collectivism. North Korea, which takes as a guiding ideology the concept of *chuche*, supports the "collectivist life view that the existence of the sociopolitical group should be valued above all rather than the life of the individual."[7] This is the concept that "mandates shift from a society based on individualism to socialism and communism or a society based on collectivism, as the historical encapsulation of human social development, in order to actualize the autonomy of a democratic society."[8] Naturally, South Korea has no related concept. The *Worker's Daily* of North Korea has severely criticized individualistic societies like South Korea by stating that the "individualistic view of life considers the highest purpose of human existence to be solely preserving one's own life with a disregard for the fate of the country and its citizens. The individuals that have this view do not hesitate to trade off their citizenship to external forces if it is for their own ease and pleasure. A life of this sort is not a life worth living."[9]

Second, with regard to culture and the arts, North and South Korea have in common an appreciation for the traditional folk arts, but North Korea adheres totally to an ideology based on the idea of *chuche*—party, class, and the people—while South Korea takes a very different stance. The late Chairman Kim Li-song defined North Korean culture and the arts as follows: "The main body of folk culture and art is rich in socialist content in its ethnic form, and will invariably contribute splendidly to the political and cultural lives of the masses."[10] "Culture and art is one of the most valuable means for educating the masses."[11] "Our new democratic arts are undoubtedly deeply thoughtful, and should be performed as a public service by the people as a weapon in conflict."[12] Of course, with culture and the arts in South Korea, diverse themes and creative freedom (as long as communism is not extolled and the art is not violent) are interdependent with the process of expanding democratization and have a wide range of expression.

Third, the characteristics of each society as a whole, and differences between them in terms of culture and the arts, are due to the economic gap and the significant differences in their approach to life. From the 1970s through the 1980s, South Korea experienced rapid economic growth and the standard of living of its citizens improved. The middle class took shape and a consumer society developed, reaching the extreme of "conspicuous consumption."[13] In Japan, there is a term *3-K*: *kitanai* (dirty), *kitsui* (difficult), *kiken* (dangerous); and in South Korea it is the 3-Ds (dirty, difficult, dangerous). In this new phase of consumerism, the social trend in the South is toward avoiding hard labor and the sweat that accompanies the 3-Ds. The society's need for the good life has become insatiable. The restaurant industry has grown rapidly with many people eating out, and individuals drive around in their own private cars. Mass media like newspapers and television are well-advanced; cell phones, beepers, personal computers, and the Internet are becoming prevalent, mainly among young people;[14] and awareness of data communication at the center of daily living seems acute in this society.

In contrast, North Korea asserts that "being a revolutionary life [sic], the most typical lifestyle expands outward within the fundamental movements of historical development," and few people lead the kind of life that characterizes South Korea. The North is not a so-called consumer society, and the talk is of food shortages rather than conspicuous consumption. For example, looking at the mass media, South Korea has about ten nationally distributed newspapers, but North Korea has only two: the party newspaper, *Worker's Daily*, and the government-owned *Democratic Korea*. With regard to television, in South Korea, seven channels can be viewed in the Seoul area if satellite stations are included, twenty-eight channels are available throughout the country via cable television, and many households watch foreign programming by satellite, such as Japan's NHK and StarTV from Hong Kong. In North Korea, there are only two channels, Korea Central Television and Manjudai Television, and television sets are not prevalent in the country.[15] Thus, quantity and quality of information encountered in daily life is significantly different for the people of North and South Korea.

The gap between the patterns of life in the two Koreas can be seen in the way holidays are spent. The actual way holidays were spent and the desired way are given on Table 1, which is based on a survey by the Korean Cultural Strategy Development Institute. In general, it shows quite different ways of spending holidays (or desired ways). "Mountain climbing," "fishing," and "traveling," which were at the top of the list for South Korea, were not even on the list for North Korea as either actual or desired holiday activities.

Fourth is the noticeable difference in language used in the two countries. North and South Korea speak the same Korean language, but there are differences in the correct writing style, seen as early as fifty years ago, such as the use of Kanji [Chinese] characters (South Korea) or nonuse of

Kanji, the method for spacing words, and inscription of compound words. This has led to a difference in orthography and the meaning of terms. For instance, (1) the entire Korean Peninsula is called Kankoku (the characters for Korea as in South Korea) in the South and Chosen in the North (the characters for Korea as in North Korea); (2) people are addressed differently ("Comrade" in the North and "Mr." or "Mrs." or "Ms.," etc., in the South); (3) foreign words introduced into the language come mainly from English in the South and from Russian in the North; (4) foreign words for geographic areas come mainly from English in the South and from Russian in the North; (5) there are subtle differences in the meaning of words—"to cultivate" (educate in the liberal arts sense) is used in the North as "to educate" (politically and ideologically); and (6) there is a movement in the North to replace the terms expressed in Chinese characters with vernacular terms.[16] Heterogeneous phenomena have developed in the spoken language, such as differences in pronunciation, rhythm, and intonation.[17] A South Korean congressional unification group says that in North Korea, a language called the "[North] Korean cultural language," based mainly on a language used in a region of North Korea, has been designated as a standard language, and fifty or more dialects differ from the language spoken in South Korea.[18] These differences are due to the ban on commerce between the two countries and differences in the political systems.[19] Also, if the language used in daily life differs, people's thinking becomes increasingly heterogeneous.

Additional differences have developed, in education, fashion, and the degree of participation in planning economic activity and government. Recently, the differences may even have extended to physical characteristics (such as average weight and height, etc.) due to the reported food shortages.

Social and Cultural Problems with Unification of North and South

If North and South Korea undergo unification or integration, what kinds of problems might this generate?

The general concepts of unification and integration should be differentiated. Unification is conceivable in various forms, and the authorities in both North and South Korea have each presented different unification models.[20] Unification scenarios using these various models will not be discussed separately because they are not directly relevant to this paper. Here, we will broadly investigate points relating to the pre-unity and post-unity integration processes.

Three possible cases should be considered: (1) unification achieved under the direction of South Korea with North and South integrated into

South Korean society, (2) unification achieved under the direction of North Korea, with North and South integrated into North Korean society, and (3) unification achieved by cooperation between North and South Koreas, with integration based on a union of the North and South. The "Peoples' Association Unification Proposal" by the South Korean government (submitted in August 1994) and "Proposal for Establishment of the Koryo Democratic Federation Republic" by the North Korean government (submitted in October 1980) approach the mutually cooperative option.

Recently, however, case 1 (North and South integration into South Korean society) has seemed to be the most likely and realistic for bringing about unification of the Korean Peninsula. It is not difficult to hypothesize the conditions that would ensue. That is, if people raised in North Korean society are to cope with South Korean society, what kinds of problems are likely to arise? We can imagine these problems by looking at those encountered recently by the increasing number of North Korean refugees entering South Korea.

The problems encountered by these refugees in South Korean society are shown in Table 2 which is based on data compiled from numerous surveys and studies done by South Korean researchers on the North Korean refugees.

The North Korean refugees have been hard hit by the various social and cultural differences between the North and South, and the psychological strain they face in South Korean society is evident. According to a survey, 68.1 percent of the refugees feel that South Korean society is more difficult than North Korean society both psychologically and spiritually.[21] It has been said that "regardless of the fact that the people of the north and south are ethnically the same, it is more difficult for the refugee to assimilate into South Korean society than it would be to integrate into the society of a completely different culture, because heterogeneity and hostility between the North and South has intensified due to the division and war lasting close to fifty years."[22]

Based on the experiences of the refugees, social and cultural problems are likely to arise in the four areas discussed below with unification or integration of North and South Korea.

First, a question arises as to whether a person habituated to the concept of the collective, as in North Korean society, would be able to cope well enough to achieve the individuation needed in an individualistic, laissez-faire society. Economic problems would be involved, and adjustments would have to be made to the capitalist system, to which competition is fundamental. This would require the introduction of market theory, the notion of personal property, and privatization of government-run companies. If individual choice and determination is introduced across the board in education, employment, and housing, all formerly managed by the North Korean government, many people are likely to become confused about how to act. In South Korea, information flows like water—through the mass media, in the newspapers and on television, by computer transmission and the Internet. It is highly doubtful that someone from North Korea, used to a single perspective on a subject and to highly edited information, could be selective when confronted with such a large volume of information, with its diverse opinions and masses of unconfirmed facts.

Second, the psychological impact of South Korean society and culture could be too great for an individual raised in the society and culture of North Korea. One shock would be the vast discrepancies between reality and the details about capitalist society and South Korean society learned in the individual's North Korean education. Some refugees "thought of capitalist society as completely corrupt, just playing and eating. They were taught that South Korean society was 'darkness,' to use a single word, a society where robbers, assailants, and con artists are roaming about, and a society where dignity and the value of the individual as well as human rights are trampled on."[23] Information concerning the outside world is restricted in North Korea, and the shock would be inestimable for an individual who, believing North Korea was a "heaven on earth," encountered capitalist prosperity. The danger of confusion, as manifested in lethargy, dissipation, and the emptiness that comes from "realizing that one's beliefs are lies and one's convictions no longer hold water," has been pointed out by psychologists, as when an individual is deprogrammed after belonging to a cult.[24] This is all the more likely in the case of unification because there is a "national religious cult" aspect in North Korea's *chuche* ideology, and a prevalence of mass agitation campaigns.[25] The shock would certainly be greater for the average citizen of North Korea, who will come to know the outside world in the process of unification, than for the refugees who had information from the outside when living in North Korea and who left of their own volition.

Another psychological shock would be complications caused by the selfish aspects of individualism in South Korea. A North Korean refugee has said: "In North Korea, one considers the welfare of others as one's own responsibility. A sense of duty and fellowship are highly valued. However, in South Korea, there is a tendency toward insincerity, even savagery, such that even if one wanted to give assistance, one assumes a blank expression as if it is not one's business. In a word, there is no compassion."[26] The accusations of selfishness, unfriendliness, and lack of discipline in South Korean society have often been pointed out by visiting foreigners as well, and will undoubtedly arouse feelings of disdain and impatience in an individual raised in North Korean culture. The profligacy of South Korean consumer society and the Western, as well as carnal, aspects of contemporary culture and art appear to be the signs of a decaying society and are abhorrent in the view of North Koreans.

Third, South Koreans have an excessive sense of superiority over the North Korean people, with strong discriminatory feelings, which may well lead to social unrest. The countries will undergo a pre-unification process and a post-unification process, but at the time of unification, unemployment will be rampant in North Korea and masses of people will flow toward the prosperous South, as was evident in the German unification process.[27] Since South Korean society tends to avoid the 3-D jobs, as mentioned earlier, large numbers of people from the north are likely to work in the south doing physical labor and simple jobs. The attitude in South Korea toward this type of employment is condescending[28] and cannot help but foster discrimination toward the people from the north. Furthermore, the South is not only in a far superior position economically, but it is more sophisticated because people from the North are ignorant of the outside world. There are also differences in physical characteristics as well as a sense of fashion stemming from more prosperous conditions in the south,[29] which are apt to increase South Korea's excessive sense of superiority and strong discriminatory feelings. That this discrimination will become mingled with regional emotions unique to South Korea cannot be denied.[30]

Fourth, feelings of mutual distrust are likely to arise between people living in the North and those living in the South. The existing differences in attitude toward politics, society, and culture of the North and South, as just described, will certainly contribute to this, but the distrust caused by the significant economic changes involved in unification will probably be an even larger problem.

At the time of unification, enormous unification costs can be anticipated, and as mentioned earlier, South Korea is assessing these. The procurement of funds to pay the unification costs is likely to come from measures to increase government revenue such as taxes, reductions in self-defense expenditures, sale of assets held by North Korea, government bonds, use of "North-South unification funds" set aside in 1990 by the South Korean government, and assistance from abroad.[31] Of course, the citizens of South Korea will be upset if taxes are increased significantly. According to a report by the [South] Korean Insurance Social Research Institute, about 30 percent of the residents of the northern Korean area will need basic support immediately after unification, and the cost of this will amount to 8 trillion, 900 billion won (about $9.7 billion) annually, or 15.2 percent of the general budget of the South Korean government for 1996. If this entire amount is paid for by taxes, the tax rate of citizens in the south will have to be raised 11 percent. In addition, if unemployed North Koreans move South, this will affect the work environment and upset laborers in South Korea. In any case, the economy of South Korea will be worsened by unification and the resentment will most likely be directed at the people of the North.

On the other hand, after the unification of North and South Vietnam, individuals from the North (or those from the National Front for the Liberation of South Vietnam) who directed the unification took over important positions in government institutions and the main corporations.[32] After unification of the Korean Peninsula, people from the South may flock to North Korea to do exactly the same thing. If so, the major movement will be South Korean corporations expanding into the North and employing North Koreans. With this kind of social structure, what will become of the North Korean elite? If treatment of the leaders and elite of the north changes after unification, a movement to reinstate the North Korean government and opposition to unification could potentially develop,[33] and social unrest after unification would be inevitable.

In addition, although as many as one million relatives long separated in the North and South will be reunited after unification, there is sufficient reason to believe confusion will result. Some members of separated families may refuse to meet with their long-separated kin, who may be rejected for various reasons (wanting to avoid property distribution, entanglements of multiple marriages, etc.) and when those who fled North Korea for the south return to claim land they originally owned.

Pre-Unification Issues for Surrounding Countries and for South Korean Society

The heterogeneity of society and culture in North and South Korea and the issues that could potentially arise because of unification have been examined. Under these circumstances, the role of South Korea, which is likely to lead the unification process, is exceedingly important in minimizing social and cultural chaos. What are the issues facing South Korean society in the future? Furthermore, how should the surrounding countries be expected to assist?

First, as a step prior to unification, South Korea should support cultural exchanges with the North. The Accord on Reconciliation Between North and South Korea as well as Mutual Exchanges and Cooperation (North-South Accord) signed by North and South Korea in December of 1991 includes an item (Article 16) on mutual exchanges and cooperation in various fields, including science, technology, education, literature, the arts, insurance, physical education, and the environment, as well as various media and publishing venues, such as newspapers, radio, television, and printed matter.[34] However, the North-South Accord has not been implemented and talks between the North and South, including those on cultural exchanges, have not progressed. The Law on Mutual Exchanges and Cooperation Between North and South Korea enacted in 1990 stipulates that approval must be obtained from the Unification Congress if South Koreans are to have contact with North Koreans (including a third country). In the eight years between June 1989, when South Korea began publishing statistics, and August 1997, contact was made on 2,377 occasions, but few of these were cultural according to the categories used by the government: 107 in the liberal arts, 54 in religion, 27 in physical education, 34 in culture, 33 in tourism and transportation, 30 in lectures and publication, 26 in science and the environment (in addition, 1,057 in economics, 942 in reunification of relatives, and 67 "other").[35] Moreover, this is a count of international events and conferences sponsored by third countries that North and South Korea attended, and different from actual cultural exchanges.

Of course, as long as North Korea does not open the gate to cultural exchanges, no progress will be made. However, it is true that under the administration of Young Sam Kim, no proposals were made to North Korea, not even for cultural exchanges. As a model, an agreement on cultural exchanges was concluded between the former East and West Germany in 1986 prior to unification, and exchanges were conducted in academics, education, the arts, movies, music, culture, and language training; between natural history museums; in the fields of preservation and publishing; between libraries; at conventions, festivals, liberal arts conferences; in radio and television; and between schoolchildren.[36]

Some form of cultural exchange is necessary to reduce the heterogeneity of the North and South and to ameliorate the cultural impact of unification on the citizens of both North and South Korea. At the time of unification, it is possible that politics and the economy will be changed suddenly by laws and regulations but, so far, "mental unity"—the unification of the structure of the psyche and consciousness founded in social and cultural influences—seems insufficiently addressed.[37] Progress in relations between the North and South on the cultural front should be no less important than political and economic talks. The former West German government, in its policies on cultural exchanges with East Germany, avoided interrupting the exchanges by keeping them separate from politics. It also set long-term objectives, and did not try to use the exchanges for short-term propaganda. The government gave its aggressive support, mainly encouraging the exchange of individuals, and made efforts to ensure that neither side lost face. Many in South Korea are of the opinion that the government should take this stance in its contact with North Korea.[38] Considering the fact that no consistency is seen in the policies of the South Korean government toward North Korea, particularly in the administration of Young Sam Kim,[39] many policies of the former West Germany should be adopted by South Korea.

Second, in order to minimize the social chaos during the unification process, South Korea should work with Japan, the United States, and China to induce North Korea to make reforms and open its doors. If North Korea moves toward reforms and allows more outside communication, the citizens of North Korea will have that much more stamina for facing a capitalist society and culture. Moreover, if North Korea improves the living standards of its people through reforms and by opening up its economy, the demands of the people will probably be diversified as they are in a capitalist society.

The public stance to date has been that the South Korean government "has made arrangements to cooperate after North Korea improves relations with allied countries such as the United States and Japan in order to establish conditions that would stabilize peace on the Korean Peninsula." (President Kim's announcement in 1988).[40] Actually, however, the government and newspaper editors have shown they are not comfortable with improvements in relations between North Korea and Japan as well as between North Korea and the United States. For example, when Japan gave assistance to North Korea in the form of rice in 1995, the South Korean government and the mass media were critical. Long-term strategies should be used to induce North Korea to reform and open up. For instance, the response to the problem of allowing Japanese spouses to visit their hometowns in Japan, the Japanese Spouse Hometown Visit Project, which started for reasons involving a single individual, has tremendous significance. It will have a large impact on the directions taken by North and South, as well as potential for bringing about change in North Korea. Then if Japan chooses to use this as an opportunity for a positive stance toward its relations with North Korea, the general situation on the Korean Peninsula should be taken into consideration, including a conference of the four parties (United States, Japan, China, Russia). "We hope that the hometown visits by Japanese spouses expand, and all who wish to can make the visit home."[41] The fact that a major South Korean newspaper stated this in an editorial should be noted for its forward-looking perspective.

Third, as part of the unification process, both conceptual and material programs should be prepared that would skillfully tailor capitalism to the people of North Korea. The existing assistance policies in the South for refugees from North Korea are criticized for having many problems. For example, (1) the assistance policies of the government are not consistent; (2) procedures are different, depending on the content of the assistance, due to arbitrary policies that make the system inefficient; (3) the focus is on financial assistance, such as special allowances (although this varies with the individual) and not on long-term assistance policies that would provide social stability; (4) the private organizations are not adequately participating and the government does not support the private groups; and (5) the assistance policies allow only for the lowest level of subsistence and there are no avenues of recourse through work or marriage.[42] Unable to adjust in South Korea, the refugees who would like to return to North Korea again have been given voice in the mass media: "South Korea is not heaven; rather, I would like to return to North Korea once again,"[43] and actually, in an incident in February 1996, a 22-year-old male refugee attempted to hijack an airplane to North Korea via China, owing to his sense of strangeness and frustration.[44]

Cases in which individuals have been enabled to adapt to a systemically different environment can certainly be seen in the example of the former East Germany after the unification of Germany and in the established policies of the Japanese government regarding returning Japanese children who were abandoned in China. In addition, examples of U.S. asylum granted to Jewish immigrants from the former Soviet Union and the asylum that various countries gave to Vietnamese refugees would provide instances of ways to cope with possible migration from north to south during the Korean unification process.[45] The various countries involved could communicate with South Korea regarding their experiences and the measures they took.

Fourth, and a very important point, not just North Koreans seeking to adjust to a capitalist society, but the people of the South will have to recognize the new situation created by unification and make an adjustment. While the number of South Koreans who feel hostile to the North is declining with the dwindling of the generation that directly experienced the Korean War, those who are interested in unification itself have also thinned.[46] According to a nationwide survey of 1,050 adults conducted in September 1996 by a South Korean newspaper, only 37.7 percent replied that "unification was absolutely necessary."[47] When unification occurs, the standard of living of South Koreans will probably be adversely affected, thus hurting the comfortable lifestyle of the South Korean middle class. For them to endure this, acclimation to the unification environment will be required. Actually, there appear to be cases at some of the South Korean universities where "North and South unification courses" are being taught both to refugees from North Korea and citizens of the South.[48]

In addition, although the two countries have a traditional ethnic culture in common, the cultural differences that have developed over the fifty-year period must be acknowledged. We have examined the various impacts the social and cultural heterogeneity of the North and South has had on the refugees. They are experiencing intercultural stress. To eliminate this stress, the people of the South must "go beyond culture," and acknowledge that using one's own culture (South) to look at another culture (North) hinders mutual understanding.[49] If one defines intercultural communication as "the mutual act performed by people with different cultural backgrounds,"[50] then means for intercultural understanding between North and South after unification are necessary. If South Korea determines that specialists are needed in North Korea throughout current society, culture, and the arts,[51] then these talented individuals could be sought to expedite mutual understanding.

Conclusion

Up to this point, this paper has discussed the extent to which the social and cultural heterogeneity has progressed in North and South Korea, what problems are likely to arise with unification due to the heterogeneity in North and South, and what South Korea and the surrounding countries should do.

The unification of the Korean Peninsula will certainly radically change the political and economic systems as well as international standing of Korea, and the chaos on the Korean Peninsula likely to be caused by the social and cultural heterogeneity of the North and South can be understood. However, there is a problem with only stressing the heterogeneity of the North and South. Ideas that "unification is impossible" or "unification is not desirable" should not be introduced.

In South Korea, as with the unification costs, general concepts like the "merits of unification" and the "cost of division" are beginning to be debated. In other words, enormous expenditures are necessary for unification, but one should also consider the merits of eliminating by unification the economic (military expenditures) as well as psychological costs incurred by the division. The mistake is debating only the unification costs while overlooking the merits of unification, and even if the unification costs are greater for a while than the merits, the merits of unification will be greater in the long term.[52] Some U.S. scholars even advocate the early unification of the Korean Peninsula because of these unification merits.[53]

In addition, although differences have developed between the North and South, there are many homogeneous aspects that are often pointed out. These would include worship of the powerful, distrust of the outsider, consciousness within the body, disregard for abuse of power, regionalism, a just sovereign-subject relationship, authoritarianism, job discrimination, priority to seniors, male superiority, racism, and a vortex social structure.[54]

If one considers the merits of unification as well as the common characteristics of North and South, the anticipated social and cultural chaos due to North-South heterogeneity may not prove to be as drastic as outsiders might imagine.

However, if one looks at phenomena such as the inability of the refugees from North Korea to adjust to South Korean society, there are bound to be more than a few social and cultural problems owing to the differences between the North and South.

Notes

[1] The Korean national textbook *Politics, Economics* for high school classes (Seoul, Dae-Han National Textbook Co., Ltd., 1997) stresses that "our race has been prospering as a single racial community based on its distinct language and heritage throughout the history of five thousand years" (page 58) and that it is a "single race." The book, *Korean History* (Part 1 of 2) by Young Jong Son, Young Hae Pak, and Yong Wang Kim (Pyung Yang, Wae Kook Moon Publisher, 1992) also indicates that "Korean citizens, who share the same racial heritage, language and culture have a history of several thousand years in one land, started from extremely early years." (page 1).

[2] Refer to *Korean History–National Standard Korean High School History Textbook* (Chang Joon So, Translated by Song Yon Ok, Meiji Shoten, 1997), pp. 67–71.

[3] *Direction of Unified Germany* by Toru Hyogo (Iwaba Shinsho, 1991), pp. 95–108.

[4] According to *Economic Expense and Benefit of Unification* by Dong Hee So and "Separation Cost and Unification Cost" by Bo Yun Kim, Dong Hee So and Min So, the major costs among the costs that have been computed are as follows: 263.2–273.6 billion dollars (Korean Development Research Institute, based on unification in the year 2000; released in 1991); 1,770 billion dollars (Chang Min Shin, based on unification in the year 2000; released in 1992); 241.5–360 trillion won (Doo Soon Ahn, based on unification in the year 1990; released in 1992); 448 billion dollars (Chin Yong Bae, based on unification in the year 2000; released in 1993); 388–841.8 billion dollars (Yong Son Lee, based on unification in the year 2041; released in 1993); and 8.67–11.29% of the Korean GNP for the initial five years and 7.47% of the Korean GNP for the following five years (Tae Gyu Pak, based on unification in the year 1995; released in 1997).

[5] *Korean Citizens' Concepts* by Takuro Suzuki (Tokyo Federation Chronicles, *Toyo*, Annex to the May 1927 issue), pp. 10–22.

[6] *Korean Geographic Tension Chronicled in References* by Hung Hwa Ko (Seoul: Sung Won, Ltd., 1989), p. 205.

[7] *For the Completion of the Leadership Revolution*, Book 5, by Jung Il Kim (Pyung Yang: Korean Labor Party Publishing Co., 1988), p. 463.

[8] *Socialism Is a Science* by Jung Il Kim, (Pyung Yang: Korean Labor Party Publishing Co., 1994), p. 2.

[9] *Labor Newspaper*, September 12, 1997.

[10] *Response to the Questions by Foreign Press*, Book 2 by Il Sung Kim (Pyung Yang: Wae Kook Moon Publishing Co., 1991), p. 99.

[11] Pages 356 357, *Selection from the Writings* by Il Sung Kim, Book 2 (Pyung Yang: Korean Labor Party Publishing, 1968), pp. 356–57.

[12] *Theory on Art of Revolutionary Literature* by Il Sung Kim (Mi Rae Co., 1971), p. 26.

[13] Refer to *Ardent Korea* by Masahiro Kuroda (Tokuma Shoten, 1993); *Korea-Watching* by Susumu Kohari (Jiji Tsushin Co., 1995); *Korea Is Changing—Life and Opinions of the New Generation* by Kyung Hoon Kim (translated by Tae Gu Yang, Aki Shobo, 1995); and *Changing Korea, Unchanging Korea* by Akira Ikehigashi (Jiji Tsushin Co., 1996) concerning the changes in Korean society.

[14] Refer to "Catch Up Effect on Consumption—Case of Durable Goods Consumption in East Asia" by Hironori Kohama, Yusuke Hirayama, Takanori Ogawa, and Kenichi Ishiwaki (*World Economics Review*, September 1997) for the propagation rate of automobiles, television, cellular phones, etc.

[15] *Theory of Film Arts* by Jung Il Kim (Pyung Yang, Wae Kook Moon Publishing, 1989), p. 12.

[16] Refer to *Media in North Korea* by Jae Chun Yoon (Seoul, Ulji Moon Hwa Co., 1989).

[17] "Introductory Korean" by Hiroomi Kanno (Shiramizu Co., 1981), pp. 283–86; and *"North and South—How to Become One* by Ho Min Yang (Seoul: Nanam Co., 1992), pp. 322–324.

[18] Refer to *Research on North and South Korean Language* by Ok Yun Lee, Hee Jin Kim, Yong Ja Kim,

and Jong Un Kim (Seoul: Do Seo Publishing, 1997) concerning the differences between North Korean and South Korean languages.

[19] "Reality of North Korea, 17 Different Languages of North and South Korea," (Seoul: Unification Seminar, 1995), pp. 2–3.

[20] Chairman Il Sung Kim stated that "For the development of Korean language, language of no nation should be accepted as is, and the language used in Seoul should not be used as the national standard because it is significantly influenced by Japanese and English. We, the core of socialism's development, must use our own distinct language as the base to develop the Korean language." (Page 10, *Selection from the Writings of Il Sung Kim,* Book 4, Pyung Yang: Korean Labor Party Publishing, 1968).

[21] At present, the government of the Republic of Korea uses Racial Community Unification Policy (proposed on August of 1994) as the basis of its unification model, while the North Korean government uses the "Koryo Race Federated Republic Establishment Model" (proposed in October of 1980) as the basis of its unification model.

[22] "Reality of Life in South Korea for the North Koreans Who Have Defected" by Hye Sung Oh (Seoul: Thesis for a Master's Degree from Seo Kang University Public Policy Program, 1996), p. 20.

[23] Refer to "Support for the Adjustment of North Koreans Who Have Defected to South Korea and the Adjustments of North Koreans After Unification" by Sang Man Lee in "Systematic Adjustment Policy for the North Koreans After Unification," from the Second System Adjustment Research Forum held in Chung Ang University, (Seoul: Chung Ang University, System Adjustment Research Center, 1996).

[24] Page 29, previously mentioned theory by Hye Jung Oh (note 22).

[25] *What Is Mind Control* by Hiroaki Nishida (Kinokuniya Shoten, 1995), pp. 210–221.

[26] Refer to "Formation of a Religious Nation in North Korea—Focus on the Technical Aspect of Mass Religion" by Hiroshi Furuta in Issue No. 20 of *Laws* (1996), and "New Paradigm of Whole" by Hiroshi Furuta shown in the "New Paradigm of Social Science," Chikuba University, Masters Program in Social Science Research (1996).

[27] Page 29, previously mentioned theory by Hye Jung Oh (note 22).

[28] Dong Chung So, a research staff member of the Korean Development Research Institute, estimates in his book *Estimated Loss of Jobs in North Korea Following Unification* (Seoul: Korean Research Institute, 1994) that "the unemployed in North Korea will reach 5,682 thousand (unemployment rate of 58.9 percent) after the unification, unless the government makes aggressive efforts. Won Bae Kim, a chief research staff member of the Korean Land Development Research Institute, estimates that the collapse of the North Korean government will lead to an unemployment rate of 25 percent (2.3 million workers) to 30 percent (2.6 million workers) of all workers, and that a minimum of 1.5 million North Koreans will migrate to South Korea within five years following unification (Han Kook Il Bo, *Korea Daily News,* November 7, 1997). Refer to *Unified Economics Theory* by Sang Man Lee (Seoul: Publishing Co., 1994), pp. 260–63, and *Conversion of North Korea's Social System and the Tasks for the Unification of the Economies of North and South Korea* (Seoul: Korean Economics Research Institute, 1996), pp. 54–58.

[29] Refer to *Moral Values and Social Awareness of Korean People* by Kyung Dong Kim (Seoul: Pak Young Co., 1992), pp. 349–394 and 567–621, for the Korean people's concept of work and labor culture.

[30] According to the statistical data compiled by The Korea Bank, South Korea's GNP as of 1996 had reached 22.4 times of that of North Korea, and South Korea's GNP per capita reached 11.6 times that of North Korea, whereas the scale of the economy is 1.9 times that of North Korea in terms of population. (*Cho Sun Il Bo* [*Cho Sun Daily News*], August 11, 1997).

[31] Refer to the previously mentioned book by Hung Hwa Ko, *Korean Geographic Tension Chronicled in References* (note 6) and to *Research on Geographical Tension* by Jong Chul Kim and Chan Jib Choi (Seoul: Han Min Co., 1991), *Research on Geographical Domination* by Yon Shin Nam (Seoul: Bak Min Co., 1991), and *Re-recognition of Korean Politics, Geographical Tension and Political Tension* by Man Hum Kim (Seoul: Bul Bit, 1997).

[32] *Unified Economics Theory* by San Man Lee, pp. 269–273.

[33] Cho Sun Il Bo, October 8, 1997.

[34] Yoshiaki Tsutsui *Vietnam* (Iwaba Shoten, 1994), pp. 194–200.

[35] "Establishment of Unified Education Policy According to Immediate Social Changes Following Unification," *Unification and North Korea's Social Culture* (Part 1 of 2) by Yong Ho Kim and Yong Pyo Hong (Seoul: Race Unification Research Institute, 1996), pp. 282–83.

[36] "North and South Meeting" No. 54, issued by Unification Institute, North & South Meeting Administrative Office (Seoul: Unification Institute, 1992), pp. 85–87. Concrete policies for cultural interchange are indicated in the sections Chapter 2, "Social and Cultural Cooperation, Interchange" of the *Annexed Agreement for the Compliance* and Chapter 3, "Cooperation Between the North and South, Interchange" of the *Agreement on Cultural Interchange, Cooperation and Non-Invasion Between North and South Korea* (signed on September 1992 following the North and South Agreement).

[37] "Monthly Updates on the North-South Cultural Interchange Efforts," No. 74 (Seoul: Unification Institute, July 1997), p. 7.

[38] "Problems and Directions of the Cultural Interchange Between North and South Korea" by Sang Chul Pak, (Seoul: *Cultural Policies Discussion,* Issue No. 8, 1997), p. 190.

[39] *50 Years Since the Division of North and South Korea—Basic Issues and Strategies for Unification*

by Sung Kil Yang, Jung Ki Lee, and Dae Jung Chang (Seoul: Nanam Publishing Co., 1996).

[40] Pages 190–193 in previously mentioned publication by Sang Chung Pak (note 38).

[41] Refer to "South Korea's Stance on North Korea Under Young Sam Kim's Administration" (*Overseas Conditions*, Vol. 43, No. 10, October 1995).

[42] Public Report "Historical Record of the 6th Republic—5-Year Administration of the President Tae Woo Ro (2) Foreign Affairs, Unification, National Defense" (Seoul, Public Report, 1992), pp. 94–95.

[43] Editorial, *Cho Sun Il Bo*, September 10, 1997.

[44] "Adjustment Support for Defecting Citizens from North Korea and Adjustment of North Korea's Citizens Following Unification" by Sang Man Lee, pp. 6–7; Yon Sei University Unification Research Institute's Research Papers (2) "Lives of Defecting Citizens—Problems and Remedies" (Seoul: Do Seo Publishing, 1996), pp. 67–77.

[45] *Shi Sa Journal* (*Current Issues Journal*) (Seoul), February 22, 1995.

[46] *Chung Ang Il Bo* (*Chung Ang Daily Newspaper*), February 8, 1998.

[47] Refer to *The Jews of Hope: The Plight of Soviet Jewry Today* by Martin Gilbert (Macmillan London Ltd., 1984, translated by Shinji Kimura, Saimaru Publishing, 1990) and *Jews in Russia* by Chizuko Takao, "Instruction, Slav World (2) Slav Races" by Teruyuki Hara (Kobundo, 1995) regarding Jews in the former Soviet Union.

[48] Refer to *Ways to Resolve the Generation Gap on Unification Issue* by Woo Young Lee (Seoul: Race Unification Research Institute, 1995). *Chung Ang Il Bo*, October 28, 1996.

> For example, Chung Ang University Racial Development Research Institute, System Adjustment Research Center. The center handles (1) support for the adjustment of refugee North Koreans living in South Korean society, (2) promotion of South Korea's awareness of the realities of North Korean society, (3) development of programs aimed to promote adjustment of North and South Koreans following future unification, and (4) support for the activities of civilian groups that provide support for the refugee North Korean citizens in South Korea. More concretely, the Center provides (1) South-North unification classes for both refugee North Koreans and South Korean citizens, (2) counseling services for refugee North Koreans, (3) human rights center for refugee North Koreans to protect human rights and to gain the world's recognition in the matter, and (4) research on the adjustment of refugee North Koreans.

[49] Refer to *Beyond Culture* by Edward T. Hall (New York: Doubleday, 1976; translated into Japanese by Iwata and Hiroshi Tani, TBS Britannica, 1979).

[50] Introduction to *Communication Between Two Different Cultures* by Ken Kamakura (Maruzen Library, 1997), p. 18; *Handbook for Communication Between Two Different Cultures* by Satoshi Ishii, et al, pp. 7–8.

[51] *Divided Nation and Unification of Culture* by Moon Hwan Kim (Seoul: Seoul University Publishing, 1994), pp. 23–27.

[52] Refer to *Political and Social Expense of Division and Benefits of Unification* by Min So and the previously mentioned "Separation Cost and Unification Cost" by Bo Yun Kim, Dong Hee So, and Min So (note 4). According to *Economic Expense and Benefit of the Unification* by Dong Hee So, when the unification cost is defined as the expenses to be incurred over the ten-year period following unification, the unification merit for the ten years between the period 1996–2005, assuming that unification took place in 1996, is 17.8 percent–27.5 percent of the previously computed unification cost, and the unification benefit amounts to the 54.9–84.8 percent of the unification cost.

[53] Refer to "Hastening Korean Reunification" by Nicholas Eberstadt, in *Foreign Affairs* (March/April 1997, Japanese translation published in *Chuo Koron*, May 1997).

[54] Refer to *Korea: The Politics of the Vortex* by Gregory Henderson (Harvard University Press, 1968, translated into Japanese by Satoshi Suzuki, Saimaru Publishing, 1973), *Understanding the Korean Race—Ties That Bind North and South* by Hiroshi Furuta (Chikuma Shinsho, 1995), and *Korean Race, Military Ruling and Financial Groups* by Akira Ikehigashi (Chuko Shinsho, 1997).

Table 1. How North and South Koreans Want to Spend Their Holidays, and Ways They Spend Them.

	How they want to spend their holidays		How they spend their holidays	
	South	North	South	North
1	Rest at home	Rest at home	Trips/Visits	Rest at home
2	Sports/Hiking	Radio/Television	Sports/Hiking	Going out
3	Walk	Veg. gardening	Cultural events	Radio/Television
4	Fishing/Picnic	Music/Reading	Fishing/Picnic/Hobbies	Film/Theaters
5	Culture Events	Going out/Sports	Instruction classes	Music/Reading
6	Reading	Movies/Theaters	Walk	Sports
7	Trip/Visits		Sports events	Veg. gardening

Research conducted by Korean Cultural Strategy Development Institute. "South" indicates the study done among South Koreans in 1994, while "North" indicates the study done among refugee North Koreans (62 members) and among those in the Chosun Clan (289 members), who previously lived in North Korea, living in Yon Byun area of China,.

[Excerpted from] pages 79–82, *Study on the Cultural Activities of North Korean Citizens* (Seoul: Korean Cultural Strategy Development Institute, 1997).

Table 2. Feelings Regarding Life in South Korean Society as Shared by North Koreans Who Have Defected to South Korea

1	They have insufficient basic knowledge concerning daily life in South Korea.
2	They are overwhelmed by the massive amount of information that is available, unimaginable in North Korea.
3	They feel discontented about the lower social status they have compared to their lives in North Korea.
4	They feel stereotyped and discriminated against by South Koreans.
5	South Koreans do not understand their Northern pronunciation, and North Koreans cannot understand words of foreign origin used in the South.
6	They cannot understand how to make, save, or spend money.
7	They feel that South Koreans lack the will to focus on problems as a group, as is done in North Korea.
8	They feel that South Koreans have the tendency to decide matters simply as black or white.
9	South Koreans seem self-involved compared with North Koreans, who have strong bonds in their relationships.
10	South Korean freedom seems immoral and corrupted.
11	Life in South Korea can be lonely without relatives, and North Koreans feel guilt about the relatives they left behind in North Korea.
12	They feel relationships among refugee North Koreans are often cautious and uneasy.
13	They miss their friends in North Korea badly when they cannot get along with the South Koreans.
14	Acts like smoking by South Korean women shocks them. But generally, they feel that women in South Korea have a higher social status than do women in North Korea.
15	South Koreans have a tendency to avoid competition.
16	South Koreans seem to expect respect for the elderly.
17	South Koreans have competitive minds and are also more obedient.
18	South Koreans seem more impulsive and are more sensitive about their pride.
19	South Koreans dislike being regulated, but are very dependent.
20	South Koreans worry about marriage. Those who were married in North Korea, in particular, have many emotional attachments.
21	They feel disappointed about South Korean lack of interest in unification issues.
22	Problems often surface in adapting to a new job and becoming enthusiastic about new labor conditions.
23	They experience difficulties in enjoying much satisfaction about the escape from North Korea.
24	South Korean society has a strong religious tendency (strict customs, clear power structure, sexual discrimination, etc.).
25	North Koreans are surprised by the low awareness of conservation and thrift.

The above list was based on "Direction of Unification Education According to the Social Changes Following the Unification" by Yong Ho Kim and Yong Pyo Hong, "North Korea's Culture and the Unification (Part 1 of 2) (Seoul: Race Unification Research Institute, 1996); "Reality of Refugee Koreans' Adaptation to South Korean Society" by Hye Jung Oh (Seoul: Seo Kang University Public Strategy Masters Program Thesis, 1996); "Support for the Refugee North Koreans Living in South Korea and the Adaptation of North Koreans Following Unification" by Sang Man Lee for Chung Ang University System Adjustment Research Center's 2nd System Adjustment Research Forum "Policy for the System Adjustment of North Koreans Following Unification" (Seoul: Chung Ang University, System Adjustment Research Center, 1996); and Yon Sei University, Unification Research Institute Research Document (2) "Lives of Refugee North Koreans—Problems and Remedies" (Seoul: Do Seo Publishing, 1996).

The Cost of Korean Unification and the Role of Foreign Investment

By Han Taejon,
Professor at the Graduate School of International Studies,
Chung-Ang University in Seoul

Introduction

After more than five decades of separation, reunification of South and North Korea (heretofore referred to as "unification") remains a top national goal in the minds of the Korean people. Although practically no Korean national under the age of fifty, whether southern or northern, has ever set foot on the other side, practically every Korean believes the peninsula must once again become one nation, as it has been for centuries past. A tune that is as familiar to all Koreans as the national anthem begins with the words "Our wish is unification."

However, when the prospects for unification became less fantastical and more concrete after the end of the Cold War, the years of blind desire and commitment to unification began giving way to practical and realistic assessments of the situation in the Korean Peninsula by the more prosperous population of the South. The swift but unexpectedly burdensome reunification of Germany—together with worsening economic conditions of North Korea, now one of the world's poorest countries—raised questions of unification cost for South Korea. Many have come to fear the potentially large financial and psychological burdens similar to those experienced by Germany.

Supporting such a perception (or driving it) are scores of studies that have reported cost projections for unification. Tellingly, nearly all of them report figures that far exceed those associated with the German experience. Filtered through the media, these studies have had a considerable impact on public opinion regarding reunification.

This paper is divided into two main sections. In the first, the question of unification cost is re-examined. In particular, the popular approach to estimating the cost is scrutinized in order to determine whether there is any theoretical content or logical consistency. In the second section, recent survey data is analyzed to gauge the current public mood regarding unification, particularly the willingness to shoulder the potential burden. We then turn to the question of what possible role, if any, may be played by foreign investment in Korea's unification process.

Studies on Unification Cost

After the sudden "collapse" of East Germany and its subsequent absorption into West Germany, the reaction in South Korea seemed to have gone from one extreme to another. In the initial stage, the speed at which the German unification proceeded raised hopes for a similar occurrence on the Korean Peninsula (in stark contrast to the general despair and fear on the part of North Korean rulers toward the possibility of being absorbed by the South). Such hopes were quickly dashed and were replaced with a growing sense of anxiety when it became clear that the revamping East German economy, which turned out to be in far worse shape than had been originally thought, was to be far more difficult than expected, threatening to place an unexpectedly severe burden on the West German economy. In 1991 alone—the first full year of unification—transfer from West Germany totaled over DM 100 billion. This comprised only a small part of a massive program to assist the restructuring of the East German economy. In the meantime, the entire German economy seemed to be suffering from the ills of rapid unification, including rising unemployment, inflation, and stagnant growth.[1]

These somber reports started to raise concerns in South Korea over the consequences of unification with the North Korea, particularly in economic terms. Discussions of the cost of unification in the Korean Peninsula began as early as 1990, with the first study appearing in 1991.[2]

The early estimates indicated that the cost of Korea's unification would be enormous and far greater than that of Germany in relative terms if the unification were to occur suddenly. All other estimates that followed were no less dramatic. As Table 1 shows, they range from $200 billion to $1.2 trillion over varying lengths of time. In order to get a better sense of the significance of these numbers, it would be useful to examine how these studies arrived at these figures.

Table 1. Estimates of Unification Cost

Source	Methodology	Definition of cost	Unification date	Result
Hwang (1993)	Income	Total investment (including private)	1990 1995 2000	$300 billion over undefined period[a] $700 billion over undefined period[a] $1,200 billion over undefined period[a]
Sang-Man Lee (1993)	German comparison	Government expenditure	2000	$200 billion over 10 years
Yeon (1994)	Income target	Government expenditure	2000	$230 billion to $250 billion over 10 years
Young Sun Lee (1994)	Income target	Government expenditure	1990	PDV $330 billion over 40 to 50 years PDV $841 billion over 40 to 50 years
Bae (1996)	German comparison	South Korean income forgone	1993	$488 billion over 5 years
Noland et al. (1996)	Income target	Government expenditure	1990 1995 2000 1990 1995 2000	$600 billion $1378 billion $3172 billion $415 billion $983 billion $2,242 billion

[a] This figure can be doubled to include the cost of socioeconomic adjustments.

Table 1.1 Some Additional Estimates (in billion $)

Source	Unification Date	Target	Period	Estimate
KDI	2000	equal income	10	372.2
RINU	–	equal income	10	438.2
Hwang, E. K.	2000	equal income	–	2,500
Jung, K. Y.	–	appropriate growth of North	32	41.2
Shin C. M.	2000	equal income	12	1,861.8
Manfred Wegner	–	German Economic Integration	5	610
British Economist Group	–	increasing North Korea's productivity to 70% of South	10	1,087.9 ~1,121.9
Harvard Univ. Institute	2000	equal income	10	250 ~500
Japan LCB Institute	1990	German Economic Integration	10	200
Far-eastern Economic Review	2000	German Economic Integration	10	40 ~300

Methodology

While the degree of sophistication and quality varies from study to study in the tools employed, the more prominent studies use a "target income" approach.[3] In order to calculate unification cost, the approach targets a per capita income level for North Korea and calculates the amount of capital transfer needed to raise North Korea's current income to that target.

A typical study is one by Noland et al. (1996). This is a useful study to focus on because of the level of attention it received in the media (the study was cited in an issue of the *Economist*).

Noland first analyzes the positive effects of liberalizing the North Korean economy using a computational general equilibrium model, which involves an array of equations that depict a set of standard general equilibrium conditions (price, quantity, income and expenditure, and market clearing). In order to highlight the effect of economic reform on the North Korean economy, quantity restrictions are imposed on the model. Using data collected from a variety of sources (with varied degrees of confidence in terms of quality), Noland conducts a simulation to test the effects of a removal of the quantity restrictions. As expected, it is found that trade liberalization would lead to output and efficiency gains, which would be magnified when total factor productivity gains resulting from technological spillovers are factored in.

However, in the short run, trade liberalization is also likely to result in the reduction of capital stock, particularly for a country like North Korea. As supporting evidence, Noland cites the study by Sinn and Sinn (1992) that reports a one-half to two-thirds reduction of the East German capital stock after unification. The loss of capital stock would tend to offset the gains from trade liberalization, and if severe enough, lead to loss in income. Noland next asks "assuming a loss of capital stock, what might be 'the level of new capital investment that would be necessary to achieve some specified income target?'" Thus, after fixing North Korea's capital stock at one-third the existing value, Noland then calculates various measures of 'new' capital needed to achieve different levels of target income, or unification costs, as shown in Table 1.

Noland's study and others have two major weaknesses that have since been pointed out and addressed analytically. The first is that most of these cost estimates are total costs and do not net out the potential benefits. The second and a related problem is that these estimates do not distinguish between expenditures that are completely forgone—and thus "costly"—and expenditures for which there is potential return—and thus should be considered investment. This distinction is highly significant. Wasteful expenditure may occur as a result of external shock and hence cannot be controlled; one must simply accept the burden and when possible, prepare for the possibility. The question of willingness to pay is completely irrelevant and only ability matters. In contrast, expenditures with potential returns—i.e., investment—is a choice variable; one may choose not only whether to undertake this expenditure or not but also how much. In this case, the question of willingness matters.

Three recent studies—Kim (1997), D. Cho (1997), and M. Cho (1997)—explicitly recognize these weaknesses and have attempted to produce new estimates. In particular, in assessing the German experience, Kim (1997) carefully distinguishes between "perishable" expenditures and investment expenditures in categorizing Germany's unification cost. For the Korean case, D. Cho (1997) calculates the cost of separation to date and provides an estimate for the benefit of unification. Recognizing the difficulty, if not the impossibility, of quantifying such benefits as increased national pride, he simply focuses on the most easily quantifiable factor, namely defense spending. Using a simple but useful method, D. Cho provides a not-too-unreasonable estimate for both the cost of separation over the past three decades and the benefits of reduced defense spending for the next several decades.

Unification Cost and Income Gap

In fairness, despite the unfortunate use of terminology (i.e. unification cost), Noland's study is an attempt to measure future capital requirement and may provide a useful guide for policy makers. On the other hand, a more serious problem with studies of this kind has to do with their qualitative conclusions, which have important policy implications. In particular, a common theme that runs through nearly all unification cost studies are the following conclusions:

- Reunification will be even more costly than for Germany because of the greater disparity in the level of income between the two Koreas.
- The longer reunification is delayed, the greater the cost (or capital requirement).

These conclusions are found in all studies that employ the income target approach. Even among the more reasonable studies by Kim (1997), one would find the claim that "Given that the difference in economic strength is greater between South and North Korea than between East and West Germany, it is not difficult to see that our economic burden, adjusted for population size, will be greater than West Germany's." Therefore, qualitatively speaking, there seems to be a tacit consensus among these studies regarding Korea's unification, especially with regard to the first point. This line of argument is based on the reasoning that for a given amount of total financial burden, per capita burden would be greater for the simple reason that the ratio of the two population in the Korean Peninsula is smaller than that of Germany.

However, this very point is, at one level, counterintuitive. Intuition would tell us that a relatively richer person would find it easier to "help" a relatively poorer person. But even without checking the intuition behind argument 1 more rigorously, it is easy to confirm that, on the basis of how the problem was initially set up by the existing studies, the first conclusion is tautological while the second is trivial. With regard to the first question, there is a logical fallacy in arriving at the preceding conclusion after posing the question of how much capital is needed to raise income. First note that asking how much capital is required to meet a target income implicitly assumes (with justification) a stable relationship between capital input and income; i.e., more capital, more income. Within the context of unification, the question posed is also equivalent to asking how much capital is needed to reduce the income disparity. *Therefore, concluding that unification would be more costly (i.e., require more capital) the greater the income gap is simply restating the question.* Since the greater cost is associated with widening income gap by assumption, the second conclusion is trivial when one assumes that the

North Korean economy will grow at a lower rate than that of South Korea, which all target income studies do.

The key lesson is that one needs to be clear about the objectives behind unification. If the objective of the economic model is simply to raise income to some target level, then such large estimates are inevitable. Certainly, equalization of income would be a desirable and perhaps even necessary objective in a unified Korea. However, it need not be a *policy* objective. A desirable policy objective would instead call for achieving self-sustained growth in North Korea. Achieving such an objective would not be just a matter of channeling massive amounts of resources into North Korea but would involve, among other things, building proper institutions and an environment for a well-functioning economy. In fact, without these conditions, the inflow of resources, i.e., capital, would likely be used inefficiently, as the experience of so many developing countries relying on aid has shown in recent history.

Unification Cost Studies and Public Attitude

While it may be fair and even useful to ask how much capital inflow would be required to raise income to a certain level, the question clearly does not address cost in any acceptable economic sense. The so-called unification costs, calculated with varying degrees of complexity, simply reflect the differences in income between South and North Korea, and cannot be considered cost at all.[4]

The issue is not merely a matter of semantics. These estimates, whatever they may be called, have had a key impact on the attitudes toward unification among South Koreans. As argued earlier, to the extent that at least some portion of the "cost" involves investment, these attitudes would matter greatly. We need particularly to pay attention to the South Korean "willingness to pay" for unification.

Willingness to Pay

One simple and useful way to gauge this willingness is to ask people directly. A recent survey by the Sejong Institute posed a series of questions on the Korean unification, including the issue of cost.[5] The responses provide a glimpse into the South Korean attitude toward the issue.

First, in order to see the general attitude toward unification itself, the respondents were given a list of tional policy objectives and were asked how much importance they attach to each one. Table 2 shows a breakdown of the responses for each objective. Although the respondents were not asked to rank the objectives, it is interesting to note that a smaller proportion of the respondents thought unification was "very important" than for nearly all other objectives.

Table 2. How Important Do You Consider Each of These Issues/Objectives? (%)

	Unimportant	Somewhat Unimportant	Somewhat Important	Very Important	Don't Know
Democratization	0.5	3.4	45.3	49.5	1.3
Nat'l competitiveness	0.8	27.6	71.3	0.3	--
Unification	1.3	10.5	43.6	43.3	1.3
Nat'l security	0.1	3.3	42.9	53.1	0.6
Foreign policy	0.1	3.0	40.7	54.5	1.7
Social welfare	0.1	2.0	30.4	67.3	0.2
Price stability	0.1	0.7	13.5	85.7	0.1
Labor relations	1.8	43.1	54.6	0.5	--
Educational reform	0.3	3.0	35.2	60.9	0.6
Environment	0.1	1.3	28.0	70.3	0.3
Traffic congestion	--	1.9	24.5	73.6	--
Corruption	0.1	0.9	24.3	74.2	0.5
Women and children	0.1	1.6	35.1	63.3	--
Social morality	0.1	0.8	29.3	69.6	0.3

The question about unification was put more directly in the following manner:

Table 3. Which of the Following Do You Agree with the Most?

Notwithstanding economic burdens, Korea must unify as soon as possible because it is the most important aspiration of the Korean people.	22.4%
Since unification can create many problems, it must proceed slowly.	70.7%
Unification is unnecessary because it would only create confusion and problems for the economy.	4.3%
Don't care about unification.	2.7%

Although those who oppose unification outright remain a small minority at 4 percent, a great majority of the respondents chose caution, which can be interpreted as a mild opposition to immediate unification. Presumably, the "problems" associated with unification would potentially include a large financial burden in the form of higher taxes. Turning to the question of willingness to shoulder this burden, the survey asked how much additional tax burden would be appropriate for reconstructing North Korea after unification.

Table 4. If the Government Were to Raise Taxes to Help Reconstruct the North Korean Economy After Unification, How Much Additional Tax Burden Would Be Appropriate?

As much as needed even if it poses burden on the economic well-being of households.	9.0%
Only to the extent that it does not burden the average household, even if the amount is insufficient to help reconstruction.	58.5%
Oppose any tax hike for unification.	28.0%
Don't know.	4.5%

Nearly nine out of ten respondents have expressed concern about the burden of additional taxes to pay for reunification, with nearly a third opposing it outright.

The responses by and large indicate a sense of ambivalence toward reunification. Support for unification itself is somewhat weaker than expected, as Tables 2 and 3 indicate. Moreover, it is highly conditional, especially with regard to the impact on economic well-being. While a majority of the respondents expressed willingness to bear additional burden associated with unification, it is severely limited. Certainly, the Korean people are not prepared to shoulder the kind of financial burden that the cost projections in Table 1 would dictate.[6] Thus, while the survey does not directly link the reports of unification cost to public attitude, it shows that the caution toward unification derives mainly from the general fear over the potential economic burden, which has been widely publicized through the media who based their reports on the unification cost studies.

The public focus on the economic burden has placed policy makers under a great deal of pressure to formulate a plan to prepare for and soften the burden. In a recent move, the government proposed establishing a unification fund to help prepare for eventual unification. With daily reports of an imminent collapse of North Korea, the proposal may have been as much of an act of publicity (to demonstrate concern) as a serious plan of action.

Whichever the case, the proposal once again demonstrated the impact of the fear of unification cost, even though the reliability of existing measures have never been seriously challenged. To be sure, it is difficult to imagine that Korea's unification would be any less of a policy challenge than that of Germany, given not only Korea's relatively weaker economic strength but also its institutions, including financial and regulatory. However, our examination of unification cost estimates indicates that the current fears may be based on misleading, or at least incomplete, analyses. It may, therefore, be useful to revisit the original source of the fear, which is the German unification.

Financing the German Unification

The concern over the burden of Korean unification first arose in the aftermath of the German unification. Such reasoning is understandable and not entirely misplaced. For one thing, the parallel between the German situation and the Korean Peninsula during the Cold War era had always invited comparisons well before the German unification took place. After the collapse of the Berlin Wall, the political climate was such that there was every expectation, indeed demand, for a full and speedy integration of East and West German political and economic institutions. The process of unification went swiftly and rather smoothly considering the complexity of the task, but it certainly did not allow enough time for careful consideration of the potential consequences. Almost as soon as the integration became finalized, it became clear that the East German economy was in far worse shape than expected and that the burden of reconstruction would be immense. Table 5 summarizes the amount of transfers to East Germany since 1991.

Table 5. Public Financial Transfers to East Germany (billion DM)

	1991	1992	1993	1994	1995	1996
I. Expenditures	139.27	265.12	213.87	185.46	159.03	155.39
1. Federal government	54.48	72.89	85.15	82.74	108.69	107.48
2. States	--	--	--	--	9.77	10.00
3. European Community	4.00	5.00	5.00	6.00	7.00	7.00
4. German Unity Fund	35.00	33.90	35.20	34.60	--	--
5. Debt processing fund (liabilities overtaken)	-0.16	64.28	9.48	1.20	--	--
6. Treuhandanstalt	23.82	57.76	53.75	30.75	--	--
7. Transfer to the state-owned housing sector	2.30	2.60	2.30	--	1.20	--
8. Old-age pension	--	4.07	7.90	10.83	16.20	19.03
9. Unemployment insurance	19.83	24.62	15.09	19.34	16.17	11.88
II. Revenue shortfall	13.09	15.41	15.50	14.22	20.28	27.35
III. Gross financial transfer (I + II)	152.36	280.53	229.37	199.68	179.31	182.74
IV. Addition revenue due to unification	22.40	27.63	30.71	36.07	40.00	42.00
V. Net financial transfer (III-IV)	129.96	252.90	198.66	163.61	139.31	140.74

* The table is from A. Boss (1997).

Table 5.1 GDP and Internal Demand in East Germany vs. Transfers from the West

	1991	1992	1993	1994	1995	1996
Gross Domestic Product	206.0	265.6	323.2	366.1	398.0	414.2
GDP minus net exports (consumption + investment)	360.4	453.6	515.6	569.4	--	--
Net exports	–154.4	–188.0	–192.4	–203.2	--	--
Transfers from West Germany	130.0	252.9	198.7	163.6	139.3	140.7
Transfers as a % of consumption plus investment	36.7	55.8	38.5	28.7	--	--
Transfers as a % of GDP	63.1	95.2	61.5	44.7	35.0	34.0
Transfers as a % of West GDP						

* The table is from A. Boss (1997).

For Korea, which has been drawing lessons from Germany in its dealings with its communist adversary throughout the Cold War, these unexpectedly large transfers were shocking.

While Germany may have provided useful lessons in the past, however, a careful appraisal of recent experience shows that the real lesson of the German unification is that paradoxically, there may be no lesson. For in the case of unification, what Korea could learn lies not so much in the similarities with Germany but rather the differences and the peculiarities surrounding the German experience that stand in contrast with Korea.

The first key distinguishing characteristic of the German unification has to do with initial economic conditions. Prior to the collapse of the Berlin Wall, it was widely believed that the East German economy was one of the strongest of all Eastern bloc countries. The economy was stagnating, but there seemed little reason not to expect a strong recovery with West German support. The West German economy was in its best shape yet historically, with sound government finances and macroeconomic indicators. These conditions help create the second peculiarity of the German case, namely a political climate highly conducive to a speedy and full integration of the two Germanys. A frequently overlooked fact concerning the German unification process is that it was democratic. Unification with the West was approved by an overwhelming majority of the East German voters in a nationwide referendum. Perhaps aided by the belief that the East German economy was relatively sound, in addition to the euphoria and a sense of national pride, the West German populace showed little signs of concern or resistance. As a result, full integration was achieved within a matter of months. In the history of nation state, such a merger is unprecedented and is nothing less than miraculous. In short, for Germany, unification was a matter of choice, not an inevitability.

The Korean situation as it stands today sharply differs on both counts. The North Korean economy today is the world's most famous basket case.

The South Korean economy itself is in transition, going through the growing pains of becoming an advanced country. Perhaps because of these conditions, political support in South Korea is not unambiguously strong and may even be waning, as can be seen from the survey results. North Korea has never had any kind of institutions for democratic referendum. In short, the kind of political climate that prevailed in Germany before unification simply does not exist in Korea today.

In this connection, it is worth re-examining the nature of the financial burden in the case of Germany. What seems to worry South Korea the most are the figures reported in Table 5—the large-scale public transfers. Here again, the difference between the Korean case and the German case is illuminating. The West German public transfer to the East consisted largely of expenditures associated with social welfare, including unemployment insurance payments and old-age pension. More important, such transfers occurred only because the West German government *chose* to provide the same welfare benefits to East Germans. In contrast, South Korea does not have the kind of generous and extensive social welfare system that Germany has. Nor can one assume that South Korea would choose to provide equal benefits to the North if and when the time arrives. Therefore, it would be misleading to use the German financial transfer to make any meaningful statements about Korea's potential burden.

The second important point about the West German transfers is that it was mostly for consumption purposes. These are the kinds of "perishable" expenditures referred to earlier that need to be distinguished from those that yield returns or investment. This is an important distinction because unlike investment, these expenditures do not contribute to permanently raising income. The West German government nevertheless made large perishable transfers presumably to serve noneconomic objectives. In the case of Korea, these objectives may not be relevant. On the other hand, to the extent that raising North Korean income is a valuable objective of unification, attention must now be turned to the latter, i.e., investment, especially from abroad.

The Role of Foreign Investment under Two Scenarios

In discussing unification cost, most studies seem to assume that South Korea must bear the brunt of the financial burden. But when the financing of unification is seen in terms of investment requirements rather than cost, the possibility for participation by other countries opens itself.

The role of foreign capital, be it debt or DFI, in economic development is well-established. South Korea itself was a main beneficiary and efficient user of large inflows of foreign capital (mainly in the form of debt). But in discussing the potential role of foreign investment in North Korea, it would be useful to consider two different scenarios: (1) unification as a gradual process, first going through economic integration then political union; (2) an abrupt event, the so-called collapse scenario.

Gradual Unification

A gradual unification process simply means that North Korea would undertake market-oriented reforms. North and South Korea would maintain their distinct political institutions, but economic barriers would eventually be lifted to the fullest extent. In effect, South and North Korea would be forming a free trade area.[7] Moreover, North Korea would become a "transition" economy, much like those in Eastern Europe. Under this first scenario, the role for foreign investment would be straightforward, i.e. investing in transition economies. If the recent trends in DFI in transition economies are any indication, then there is reason for optimism in the case of a reform-oriented North Korea.

Table 6. FDI Inflow into Selected Central and Eastern European Countries (million US$)

	Inflows					Stock	
	1991	1992	1993	1994	1995	1994	1995
Czech Republic	--	--	654	878	2,500	2,508	5,008
Hungary	1,462	1,479	2,349	1,144	3,500	6,434	9,934
Kazakhstan	--	100	150	185	284	435	719
Poland	291	678	1,715	1,875	2,510	4,879	7,389
Romania	40	77	94	340	373	551	924
Ukraine	--	200	200	159	200	559	759

Source: *World Investment Report 1996*

The Collapse Scenario

The most important concern under the collapse scenario is the potential for massive migration of North Korean population to the South. As argued in previous sections, all other concerns with unification involve how to reconstruct the North Korean economy, which is ultimately about how to boost productivity, and which is in some sense controllable. But the massive migration represents potential negative shock to the South Korean economy, which may be out of the control of the policy makers. Clearly, as the responses to the following Sejong survey indicate, the South Korean people are well aware of and concerned about this potential problem.

Table 7. If the North Korean Regime Collapses and North Koreans Attempt to Migrate to the South in Mass Numbers, How Should This Be Dealt With?

Accept without any restrictions.	14.3%
Establish restrictions to limit their number.	57.3%
Do not accept any for the time being.	21.7%
Don't know.	6.7%

Before analyzing this problem, it is necessary to begin by clarifying the meaning of "collapse." In economic terms, one may as well conclude that collapse has already taken place in North Korea. The de facto economic collapse has led many pundits to predict political collapse. But it should be remembered that historically, even the most dire economic conditions have not necessarily induced major political changes, much less a collapse. Examples include Cuba and many African countries. Moreover, many North Korean watchers maintain that the current political class has successfully established a firm grip on power. But even supposing that the current leadership is replaced by another, this need not imply a collapse of the entire regime. Presumably, the new leadership would have the support of key actors, including the military, and hence control over domestic affairs. If this new leadership undertakes reform, then the arguments for the first scenario would apply.

The concern over the collapse of North Korea is actually related to two possibilities. First, the new leadership is hostile but instead of keeping its border closed, it attempts to sabotage the South by deliberately opening its borders to the South and sending its poorest population to settle in the South. However unlikely this scenario may be, it is not without precedent; Cuba once accepted the dare of the United States to send all "unhappy" Cubans to U.S. territory. Alternatively, under the worst case scenario, the new leadership simply loses domestic political control, resulting in anarchy. However, unlikely and short-lived anarchy may be, massive migration may ensue.

The question then is, under these extreme scenarios would it be technically possible for South Korea to prevent migration? There are two possible solutions. The first involves physical force, which is say that South Korea would maintain its heavily fortified border to the North. Moreover, any North Koreans making their way to the South would be considered "illegal aliens" and be sent back. Despite the concern over massive migration expressed by South Koreans, such a policy is unlikely to be politically popular or acceptable.

A second and more feasible option involves economic incentives. As discussed earlier, the West German strategy has been to make massive transfers to the East. The primary underlying motive was presumably to prevent a massive surge of East Germans to the West. As has been pointed out already, this may not be the best option for South Korea. Under the worst case collapse scenarios, South Korea may have no choice but to make some allowances. If the new North Korean leadership has sufficient control over the border, South Korea could simply offer a "bribe" to maintain that control. Complete anarchy is a far more serious concern. But anarchy is never long-lasting. Some form of political order would be restored, possibly by the leadership in the South. Then the immediate task in controlling southern migration would be twofold: first, given the current state of the North Korean economy, to provide immediate relief; second, to begin immediate reconstruction. The first task would require transfers from the South, but these need not be massive as the objective would be to provide sustenance and basic necessities. (Recall also that South Korea lacks a comprehensive social welfare system.) The second task, on the other hand, would require capital, likely in massive quantities, which Korea alone could not supply.

Clearly, in the initial stages, South Korea would be the primary injectors of capital into the North Korean economy. But eventually, the "unified" Korea would want to (as opposed to "have to") look to overseas sources of investment. Of these potential sources, Japan stands out as the most promising candidate. Japan's record of direct foreign investment in developing countries is well-established. In particular, Japanese investment has provided the engine of growth for many countries around Southeast Asia. In the case of North Korea, it is clearly in line to become the major investor. This would depend on whether proper conditions would eventually prevail, which is up to the task of the South Korean political leadership. Should a political union in the Korean Peninsula occur suddenly under South Korea, the immediate task for the government would be to create the proper environment for DFI. In particular, the government must be ready to quickly establish the most basic regulatory and institutional structure.

Because of the overemphasis on the potential problems related to unification, it has been too easy to overlook the potential opportunities and benefits of unification. In many ways, North Korea resembles the South in the early 1960s: desperately poor and backward but rich in educated manpower. While aid from richer countries was helpful, no one would argue that such transfer was responsible for South Korea's economic growth and development. Like all other fast-growing countries, it relied on the injection of foreign capital, which it put to productive ends with spectacular success. North Korea will be no exception.

Notes

[1] See also *United Germany: The First Five Years.*

[2] As far as the author can tell, the very first was an unpublished manuscript by Ki Woo Shik, "The Cost of Unification."

[3] The other commonly used approach is the "German comparison" approach. Korea's unification cost is derived by simply extrapolating the actual German expenditures taking into account differences in population, income, and other factors.

[4] In strictly economic terms, pure cost calculations would need to involve welfare considerations. In the case of Germany, pure cost of unification would be associated with the welfare losses emanating from the macroeconomic shocks, including output loss and high unemployment. For a welfare analysis of Korean unification, see Han (1997).

[5] *National Survey of Public Opinion 1997 (Kukmin oeshik chosa 1997)* is an annual survey conducted by the Sejong Institute that polls the public on a wide range of issues, including domestic politics, foreign policy, and economic policies.

[6] Here again, it is difficult to see the utility of cost projections that yield amounts that taxpayers are simply unwilling, and most likely unable, to bear.

[7] It is important to distinguish this relationship from a customs union like the EEC, which allows free movement of not only goods and services but also factors of production, especially labor.

The Diplomacy of German Unification:

Lessons for Northeast Asia

By Gary L. Geipel,
Senior Fellow, Hudson Institute

Three assumptions underlie this analysis: (1) The present division of Korea into ROK/DPRK will not persist forever; indeed, change appears quite likely in the coming decade. (2) Military-strategic stability in Northeast Asia will be greater and economic aspirations more likely to be fulfilled if a unified or confederated Korea avoids both domination by China and a completely independent security posture. (3) When change arrives on the Korean Peninsula, it is likely to force a quick succession of vital diplomatic and military decisions; therefore, *now* is the time to discuss and to begin to establish a foundation for Korea's security posture after the disappearance of the DPRK.

The other conference contributions elaborated the foregoing assumptions. This presentation will extract lessons for northeast Asia from the recent diplomatic history of Germany's unification. In the period 1989–1990, Germany achieved unification and full sovereignty without creating strategic instability or provoking military buildups in Europe. Indeed, German unification coincided with the end of bloc-to-bloc confrontation in Europe and a large-scale demilitarization of Central Europe. The model of Germany's unification cannot be carried over unchanged into Northeast Asia; there are many differences of culture, history, existing international frameworks, and personalities between the regions surrounding Germany and Korea. Nevertheless, numerous surprising similarities do exist.

Forces inside West Germany (FRG) and earlier models of German diplomacy might have led the FRG to pursue a posture of neutrality and/or strategic independence in 1990 as the assumed price of unification. The progress of European integration and therefore the economic security of Western Europe almost certainly would have been put at great risk by such developments. Similarly, internal pressures and the weight of history could lead ROK leaders to accept PRC dominance and/or to seek the removal of U.S. forces from Korea as the assumed price of the DPRK's disappearance. Northeast Asian security and the region's economic progress could be put at risk by such developments.

In Western Europe, the leaders of Britain and France expressed great anxiety in 1989–1990 at the prospect of German unity, and if their preferences had prevailed, they would have worked to continue Germany's division at the risk of strategic ambiguity and instability in Europe. Similarly, Japan may attempt to prolong Korea's division and relative weakness as a misguided form of insurance against regional competition.

The possibility of German unification arose at the same time as East Germany's communist patron, the Soviet Union, faced an internal crisis regarding its economic and political order. German unification might have brought about a dangerous, imperial reaction by the Soviet Union. In Asia, the possibility of Korean unification will coincide with continued internal confusion in China over the nation's economic and political evolution. The disintegration of the DPRK, China's buffer against Western influences, could bring about a dangerous, imperial reaction by the PRC.

Principled and self-confident diplomacy by the United States and West Germany in 1989–1990 not only avoided the disastrous possibilities just outlined but achieved outcomes close to the maximum goals of those two countries. In Northeast Asia, the same kinds of players will have an interest in the outcome of Korea's transformation (see the attached chart) and "maximum goals" can be laid out that look very similar to what was achieved in Europe: To bring about the confederation or unity of the divided nation (Germany ⇒ Korea) with the acquiescence of the continental power (Soviet Union ⇒ PRC) but without increasing the influence of the continental power, while at the same time promoting greater regional cooperation among free-market democracies (Britain/France/Germany ⇒ Japan/Korea), improving the prospects of wider regional integration (to Poland/Eastern Europe ⇒ Russia), easing suspicions about former expansive military powers (Germany ⇒ Japan), and signaling the importance of national sovereignty and self-determination in the region (to Eastern Europe/former Soviet republics ⇒ Taiwan).

In Northeast Asia, as it was in Europe, the role of the United States will be very important in achieving those maximum goals: (1) As a semi-outsider, the United States can act as the trusted "honest broker" in diplomatic relations between nations with long histories of antagonism. (2) The United States is the only player with the military power to counterbalance the weight of the PRC; therefore, alliance with the U.S. is the surest and perhaps only means for the ROK to negotiate with China from a position of strength. (3) A U.S. military presence in the region eases or eliminates pressures on Japan, Korea, and even China to increase their own military preparations against the others. (4) The credibility of U.S. support for Taiwan and of long-standing U.S. efforts to control maritime disputes in Asia will be evaluated with reference to America's Korea policy in the years ahead.

As important as the U.S. role may be, the earlier experience with German unification teaches that the achievement of maximum goals in Northeast Asia will depend on several factors beyond the mere presence of U.S. forces and diplomats: (1) Diplomacy surrounding the transformation of Korea must *not* be open-ended, just as U.S. diplomacy in Europe did not leave open the possibility of German unity outside the North Atlantic Treaty Organization (NATO). (2) Early trilateral political and military cooperation between the United States, Japan, and ROK could establish a unified posture toward China not unlike the unified posture represented by NATO and the European Union during the course of German unification. (3) The ROK must not be bypassed in U.S. negotiations with the DPRK or China over the future status of the peninsula, just as West Germany was not bypassed in U.S. negotiations with East Berlin and Moscow. (4) Japan's economic power can be harnessed to improve the prospects of the former DPRK and to reassure Korea regarding Japan's intentions, just as Germany's economic power (for example, its private investments in Eastern Europe and its massive payments to the Soviet Union in exchange for troop withdrawals) played a constructive role in securing Europe's peace. (5) U.S.–Japanese-Korean diplomacy toward China must be firm but face-saving, as was Western diplomacy toward the Soviet Union in 1990 (for example, preserving the territory of the former DPRK as a buffer into which no non-Korean military forces may be permanently deployed would be similar to NATO's pledge of no deployments into the former East Germany).

Japan & Germany

New Players, Similar Roles?

Northeast Asia today		Europe in 1989–91
	The unifying countries . . .	
ROK	⇒	Federal Republic of Germany (FRG)
DPRK	⇒	German Democratic Republic (GDR)
	The unstable and possibly aggressive continental power . . .	
PRC	⇒	Union of Soviet Socialist Republics (USSR)
	The anxious, Western-oriented economic power(s) . . .	
Japan	⇒	Britain and France
	The countries struggling to assert and maintain sovereignty . . .	
Taiwan	⇒	Eastern Europe and (then-soon-to-be) former Soviet republics
	The anxious bystander . . .	
Russia	⇒	Poland
	The superpower with military forces in the region . . .	
USA	⇒	USA
	The historic "unsatisfied military" power, now a global economic power . . .	

About Hudson Institute

Organization

Hudson Institute is an internationally recognized public policy research organization that forecasts trends and develops solutions for governments, businesses, and the public. Founded in 1961 by the late Herman Kahn, the Indianapolis-based not-for-profit 501(c)(3) organization has more than seventy researchers and employees.

Organization Focus

Unlike most public policy institutions, Hudson is strong in both domestic and international issues. Its Midwest location offers a clear vantage point on the grassroots of American society while its satellite offices help develop and communicate its findings and messages to national and international businesses and governments. Hudson Institute advocates and implements a practical approach to public policy research. Such efforts require going into the field to complete research and offering technical assistance to various industries and institutions. Hudson is a nonpartisan futurist organization that is known for its healthy skepticism of conventional wisdom and its guarded optimism about solving tomorrow's problems today.

Founder

Herman Kahn, along with Max Singer and Oscar Ruebhausen, established Hudson Institute as a research organization dedicated to thinking about the future from a contrarian point of view. From 1961 to 1983, Kahn maintained—and depended on—a research staff committed to engaging in intellectual exchange and analysis that offered predictions about the future. Trained as a physicist, Kahn applied his skills and unconventional thinking to examine issues in economics, national security, and international affairs. Since his death, Hudson Institute has continued to conduct research that reflects Kahn's interest in the future while addressing the most significant challenges facing America and the world.

Today's Leaders

Herb London, Ph.D., a widely published social critic and the John M. Olin Professor of Humanities at New York University, became president of Hudson Institute on September 1, 1997.

Curt Smith, a former journalist and Capitol Hill aide, serves as vice president and chief operating officer.

Ed Rubenstein, an economic consultant and journalist, is director of research.

About the Contributors

Gary L. Geipel is Senior Fellow at Hudson Institute.

Kim Taehyun is at the Graduate School of International Studies, Chung-Ang University in Seoul.

Hattori Tamio is Professor of Comparative Sociology at Doshisha University in Kyoto.

Han Taejon is Professor of International Relations at the Graduate School of International Studies, Chung-Ang University in Seoul.

Kohari Susumu is Research Associate at the Faculty of International Relations at the University of Shizuoka.

Lee Sook-Jong is Senior Fellow at the Sejong Institute in Sungnam City, Korea.

Murooka Tetsuo is Associate Professor at the National Institute of Defense Studies in Tokyo.

Akihisa Nagashima is Adjunct Senior Fellow in Asian Studies at the Council on Foreign Relations and Visiting Scholar of the Edwin O. Reischauer Center for East Asian Studies at the Johns Hopkins School of Advanced International Studies (SAIS). He previously served as Chief of Staff at the Office of Representative.

Otsuka Umio is Commander, Japan Maritime Self-Defense Forces and currently serves on the Maritime Staff Office in Tokyo.

Robert Dujarric is Research Fellow, National Security Studies Department, at Hudson Institute in Washington D.C.

Yamaguchi Noboru is Major General, Japan Ground Self-Defense Forces and currently serves as defense and military attaché in Washington, D.C.

About the East Asian Security Study Group

The East Asian Security Study Group is a private study group formed in 1996. The group carries out research projects from time to time in regard of security issues in Northeast Asia centering on the Korean Peninsula.

Chairman: Hajime Izumi, Professor, University of Shizuoka.

On December 5-6, 1997, Hudson Institute and the East Asian Security Study Group held a conference on Japanese-Korean relations.

In the two and a half years since the symposium took place, the pace of the improvement of Korean-Japanese relations has been dramatic. The papers presented at the conference will give interested observers the opportunity to understand the background to the development of relations between Japan and Korea.